*". . . building professionalism
in project management . . . "*

A FRAMEWORK
for Project and Program Management
INTEGRATION

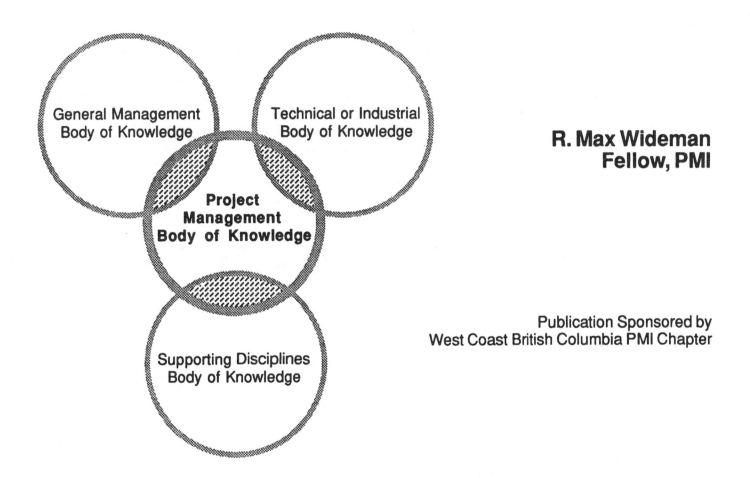

**R. Max Wideman
Fellow, PMI**

Publication Sponsored by
West Coast British Columbia PMI Chapter

**Preliminary Edition
for Trial Use and Comment**

The PMBOK Handbook Series – Volume No. I

A publication of the Project Management Institute

The Cover

One of the characteristics of a profession is that it has a unique and identifiable body of knowledge. The PMBOK (Project Management Body of Knowledge) has been developed to identify the body of knowledge for this profession. The figure on the cover serves to illustrate that the PMBOK intersects with three other distinct bodies of knowledge, all four of which the project manager (PM) must possess to one degree or another. Two of these are singular in nature, the PMBOK and the General Management Body of Knowledge. Each of the other two actually represent sets of knowledge. For example, on a given assignment, the PM may have to interface with, if not integrate the efforts of, a variety of industries, technologies, and supporting disciplines. While specific expertise in each of these is not required, and may be dysfunctional, it is desirable for the PM to have a basic vocabulary in each in order to facilitate communication. Chapter IV provides a discussion of the PMBOK relative to the other bodies of knowledge.

Indeed, the position of the PMBOK in this diagram illustrates one of the dominant roles of the PM and the focus of this handbook, that of integrator of all efforts on the project to aid in achieving the objectives of the project in the most expeditious manner.

PMBOK Handbook Series

The "PMBOK Handbook Series" of publications by the Project Management Institute (PMI) is an official document in support of the PMBOK. Handbooks are first issued as a "Preliminary Edition for Trial Use and Comment" as is the present document. After due time has lapsed for interested parties to submit their reactions and comments, these reactions will be considered and incorporated as appropriate. At that time, the handbook is re-issued without the proviso.

The PMBOK is the official body of knowledge from which questions are derived and used in the examinations as a part of the Project Management Professional certification program of PMI.

This Book

All correspondence and inquiries should be directed to:

Project Management Institute
130 South State Road
Upper Darby, PA 19082
(610) 734-3330

Library of Congress Cataloging-in-Publication Data

Wideman, R. Max.
    A framework for project and program management integration / R. Max Wideman.
        p.   cm. — (The PMBOK hanbook series; no. 1)
    Includes bibliographical references.
    ISBN - 1-880410-01-X (Volume 1)
    1-880410-00-1 (10 Volume Set)
    1. Industrial project management.   I. Title.   II. Series.
    HD69.P75W53 1991
    658.4′04—dc20
                                                          91-28160
                                                          CIP

ISBN   1-880410-01-X (Volume 1)
       1-880410-00-1 (10 Volume Set)

Manufactured in the United States of America.

Foreword

In an increasingly complex and competitive business environment, experience has shown that the following are critical to success:

- The ability to properly envision and clearly define goals,
- The ability to develop financially sound and timely strategies, and
- The possession and/or acquisition on the knowledge, interpersonal skills, and tools needed for successful implementation.

Project management professionals are doers, achievers, and leaders. These characteristics are the hallmarks of Project Management and the reason Project Management is flourishing as the most effective management system for a world of change.

The Project Management Body of Knowledge (PMBOK) was developed as a document in 1988 in response to the need to identify and describe the major knowledge areas—the framework—of project management. Through the contributions of PMI members—both successful practitioners and seasoned academicians, the Project Management Body of Knowledge was developed to encompass not only the basic knowledge and technical definitions of Project Management but also its complexities, strategies, and tactics.

This handbook is the first of PMI's educational publications designed specifically to complement PMI's Project Management Body of Knowledge. It provides a general explanation of project management and its value, some insights into its processes, and suggestions on how to manage projects to achieve greater success. As such, I hope that this handbook will appear to a number of people; from those who are looking for a summary of the basics of project management to those who are studying for PMI's Certification Program, as well as project management short-course developers, trainers, and academics.

This handbook is also intended to be one of a series, subsequent issues of which will cover the content of the PMBOK in each of its functional components. It is being published now as a "Preliminary Issue" for trial use and comment, and I hope that fellow members will take the time to read it and offer constructive suggestions and industry examples which can be used to improve and upgrade the subsequent issue. I believe this input is especially important since the subject matter is tied specifically to PMI's official PMBOK, a body of knowledge which is constantly evolving.

One of the special features of this handbook is that it has been created entirely by the volunteer effort of many members of the Project Management Institute. An effort such as this involves countless hours of individual research and writing as well as the coordination and integration of these volunteer contributions. I am deeply appreciative of the team of PMI volunteers whose generosity of time and creativity have made this possible. On behalf of PMI, congratulations and thank you!

Mary Devon O'Brien, PMP
President

Preface

Welcome to the exciting world of project management! Whether your interest is in small administrative projects, management projects, large-scale capital works, or a whole program of projects; whether project managers report to you or managing a project is your chosen career or just a short-term obligation; whether your project is public, private or personal; PMI welcomes your interest. PMI hopes that this handbook will provide the reader and the student of project management with some fascinating insights into the expectations, processes and satisfaction of managing projects successfully. By managing project responsibility through effective practices and incentives—essential prerequisites for project success—project management captures the synergies and focus of people working together with a clear common goal and, consequently, greater job satisfaction.

Perhaps the first step is to recognize that learning about project management is learning about a process—the process of managing change. Not just any sort of change, of course, because change is going on all the time. No! The issue is change which is carefully conceived, deliberately planned and expertly executed—all for someone's benefit. In short, the effective management of creative and beneficial change.

Records of major projects abound since early history. They have always been managed for better or worse, by design or default, according to the skill, intuition, and luck that the manager could muster at the time. But today we live in an age of unprecedented change, which must be actively and carefully managed for our very survival. Therefore, there has been a growing recognition that management, and particularly project management, requires special skills which are essentially different from the technical skills required for the project in question. Indeed, there are aspects common to all projects which are quite outside the scope of these technical areas, but which must be managed every bit as carefully if the final outcome of the project is to prove successful.

Project management is currently experiencing an upsurge in interest and application. More and more, it is becoming central to the conduct of business—as an essential strategy for managing constructive change. Senior executives and managers who wish to accelerate their alignment with today's hectic pace of evolution should focus on this emerging discipline as the way to achieve their goals.

This handbook deals in a general sense with project management and its integrative aspects. As can be seen from the sectional end-notes, its contents have been drawn from many sources, generally originating from PMI members, or from thoughtful comments contributed specifically for this work.

It is hoped that the reader will find this handbook informative, stimulating and most helpful reading.

Acknowledgments

From the very beginning, PMI members have been highly enthusiastic about identifying that body of knowledge which is significant and unique to managing projects successfully. Over the years, many individuals have contributed their knowledge and experience to this venture with the result that a steady improvement has been seen in our understanding of this emerging profession. First came the development of Ethics, Standards and Accreditation criteria, followed a few years later by the consolidation of project management knowledge under the published title Project Management Body of Knowledge (PMBOK).

Recognition of this publication has led to the development of a set of PMI handbooks expanding the PMBOK document, and these would be especially useful for PMP certification candidates. Once again, a group of PMI members are enthusiastically volunteering their time to complete this endeavor.

I would like to thank all those who have contributed both directly and indirectly by their comments, conversations, reviews and suggestions, at seminars, presentations, lectures and meetings, too many to cite all by name. I would, however, like to mention a few who have been particular contributors or my mentors in this effort: Philip Nunn, for his insight and encouragement; Lloyd Rogers, for an overlooked conversation some years ago; Bob Youker for his early work and recent observations on "environment"; Bill Duncan, Jeff Pinto and Shakir Zuberi for their written contributions; and lastly, Chris Quaife and Alan Stretton, not only for their contributions, but also for their thorough critiquing and suggestions as to form and content of this important document. I am sure that readers will benefit greatly from their work. Any errors or omissions, however, are my responsibility.

Throughout, my wife Audrey has been most supportive of this work and has not only reviewed much of the manuscript in a most helpful way, but has also given unfailing encouragement and advice in tackling some of the technical aspects of producing a text such as this.

R. Max Wideman, Fellow, PMI
Editor

Dedication

To the West Coast B.C. PMI Chapter
My friends and supporters who have pointed the way.

Contents

Part A Project Management

Chapter I INTRODUCTION

Chapter II Definition and Content of Project and Program Management

Part B Project Structure

Chapter III The Project Life Cycle (PLC)

Chapter IV Modeling Project Management

Part C   Project Dynamics

Chapter V   Project Environment I - Internal Interfaces

Chapter VI   Project Environment II - External Interfaces

Chapter VII   Project-Oriented Controls

Chapter VIII   Towards Successful Project Management

Part D   Conclusions

Chapter IX   Summary and Conclusions

Appendices

A.   A Historical Perspective

B.   Establishing PMBOK Terms Of Reference

C.   Project Management Applications

D.   Project Management Learning

E.   Glossary Of Primary Terms

Illustrations

Part A   Project Management

Chapter I   Introduction

A. Why Project Management is Needed[1]

A Common Thread runs through all of the following examples of real-life successful undertakings:[2]

- Planning, financing, designing, building, opening, operating or leasing institutional, commercial, industrial, or infrastructure facilities in most major population centers in recent years;
- The completion of a major refinery revamp, upgrade and expansion at Texas City to meet a previously agreed schedule and budget without crippling the existing refinery operations;
- Successes in the NASA program at the Johnson Space Center;
- Open heart surgery operating room practices that now get the patient out in about half the time with greatly reduced stress for the team;
- The development, production and distribution of a major new product, including accompanying advertising and sales program, by a well-known software/hardware company; and
- The resounding success in logistics, efficiency, administration, responsiveness and execution reflected in the Houston Economic Summit meeting of seven nations.

What is the common thread? All of these real-life endeavors were projects managed successfully by the concepts, techniques and practices embraced by the Project Management Institute. Indeed, the value of the concepts and practices advanced by PMI have been documented over recent years and proven again and again. The reader should refer especially to the published Showcase Projects, in-depth case studies of actual project successes and failures, which appear regularly in PMI's *PM NETwork* magazine.

Projects have always needed managing, yet many just limp along at a fraction of their potential simply because people don't know how to make them run any better.

Project Management is of Value to any organization determined to manage such change efforts successfully and to all those who are required to implement corporate strategy and the transitions necessary to keep pace with the evolution of the modern world. It is therefore of interest from the first line manager to the chief executive.

The Special Features of Projects demand that projects receive explicit management attention, whatever their nature, size and duration. Features, some or all of which may be exhibited by a project, can be identified as follows:

- **Rarity**
  - ☐ The definition of the project's end objectives (scope) makes it a unique or relatively infrequent undertaking

- **Constraints**
  - ☐ Limited time (i.e., specified start and finish)
  - ☐ Limited money (i.e., specified budget)
  - ☐ Limited resources (e.g., people, skills, equipment and materials)

- **Multidiscipline**
  - ☐ The contributing efforts of more than one organization may require integrating
  - ☐ The work of more than one discipline may need coordinating across organizational boundaries
  - ☐ Several skills may require careful coordination

- **Complexity**
  - ☐ Managerially complex due to objectives conflicting with constraints
  - ☐ Opposing individual objectives of many parties, both internal and external, may require managing
  - ☐ Technology may be changing in methods and approach
  - ☐ The technology itself may be complex

- **Dynamic Response**
  - ☐ Visibility of project as an agent of change
  - ☐ Responsive to external changes during the life of the project
  - ☐ Responsive to internal developments reflected by the project life cycle

- **Other Factors**
  - ☐ An appreciation of the effect of the project on the participating organizations; and environment is crucial
  - ☐ Substantial sponsor commitment is needed
  - ☐ A broader-based understanding of the technology is required
  - ☐ Appropriate technical skills must be found
  - ☐ Day-to-day issues must be dealt with in a timely manner
  - ☐ Effective project management expertise is essential

The Benefits of Effective Project Management are now gaining greater recognition and project management is playing a much more central role in the mainstream management of successful companies. Why? Because changes in the global marketplace are becoming commonplace, and organizations face growing competitive pressures in an unforgiving arena.

The use of project management techniques in developing both products or services and the processes (i.e., marketing, procurement, manufacturing, quality and after-sales services, etc.) required to get those products or services to the customer on a more timely basis is increasingly critical.[3] Senior managements increasingly recognize the advantages of flatter, more fluid, team-based approaches in dealing with the really important issues, especially those that cut across the organization as a whole.[4] So instead of being geared only to occasional special assignments, project management is set to become a way of business life.

B. The Potential for Project Management[5]

Growth, change and projects go together. In an increasingly turbulent world in which business becomes faster paced, more complex and more competitive, so the rewards go to those organizations which are more flexible, more in tune with their customers' wants, more focused on their main product or service, and more professional in every aspect of their business.

Modern project management specifically sets out to deal with this situation. With flexible project teams and resources focused on the needs of the enterprise, project-based planning and implementation aligns corporate strategy and effort. Managing projects helps to develop those qualities of initiative and effectiveness that senior management looks for in advancing its organization. Indeed, two of the largest project management organizations in the world, PMI and INTERNET, share a strong perception that the creative concept of project management is universal and generic, crosses all cultural, national and linguistic barriers, and many of the problems inherent in creating change or adapting to change are common to all.[6]

Some corporate cultures are much more supportive of project working than others, and top managers who plan to introduce the project management discipline, or who wish to improve existing project performance, must pay attention to cultural, structural, practical and personal elements. Project management requires team-working skills, rather than rigid functional divisions, and values quality information, discipline and goal-orientation. Its primary focus is on what has yet to be done, and who will do it, rather than on records of past achievements. It is as much about attitudes and motivation as it is about procedures, tools and techniques.

For project management to succeed and its benefits to be realized, three ingredients must first be in place. These are: support from senior authority; agreement and commitment at the level of responsibility; and, a willing acceptance at the level of impact.[7] As Konosuke Matsushita, Executive Director of Matsushita-Electric, observed in comparing Western and Japanese management styles: "...for us, the core of management is precisely the art of mobilizing and pulling together the intellectual resources of all employees...only by drawing on the combined brain power of all its employees can a firm face up to the turbulence and constraints of today's environment."

Project managers are often selected for the extent of their technical competence alone. This can be a mistake. Certainly, he or she needs to know enough about the technical nature of the project at hand to be able to separate the real issues from the red herrings. But the primary areas of competence required by any project manager include: communication; the ability to get the best out of the real specialists; leadership and decision-making skills; and planning and forecasting. In fact, the very stuff of future senior management!

Nevertheless, project management should not be used until the leaders of the organization are committed to its use and are willing to prepare a suitable culture for project management to germinate and grow.[8]

C. The Need for Professionalism in Project Work

Except perhaps for those projects undertaken by a single person on a voluntary basis, the idea of setting out to achieve certain predetermined objectives in several concurrent areas presupposes the application of discipline and control through sound management practices. This usually requires delegation of effort to various specialized groups through whom the separate objectives are to be achieved, matched by professional coordination to offset potential fragmentation.

The more vital or urgent the endeavor, and the more complex the situation, the more important it is to have the project managed by competent effective entrepreneurial leadership if the project is to succeed according to expectations. Such leadership involves knowing what has to be done, how to do it, when to do it; but perhaps most importantly, how to deal with the people who will get it done. Such is the mark of a true professional!

D. Attributes of a Profession

Since the late 1970s, there has been a significant effort by PMI members to develop project management into a recognized profession. By examining such callings as accounting, engineering, law, medicine, and so on, a study by PMI established that there are five essential attributes that are generally associated with a recognized profession. These are:[9]

A Unique Body of Knowledge which implies the existence of principles and concepts that are unique to the particular profession, and which can be codified and documented so that they may be studied and learned through formal education;

Supporting Educational Programs which define the minimum level of entry to a recognized educational process leading to a progressive career path;

A Qualifying Process which sets and promotes the standards for professional designation;

A Code of Ethics which makes explicit what is considered to be appropriate behavior and which is used to self-police unprofessional behavior, and hence limit the necessity for direct legal intervention;

A Supporting Organization which acts as the self-policing agency, and reflects a desire on the part of its membership to commit time, money and energy towards self-improvement, to publish research and experience to enhance the body of knowledge, and generally to work towards a better understanding of its purpose on the part of the public and the profession itself.

In addition, a number of characteristics of a professional organization have been identified.[10] A professional organization:

- Promotes public interest and awareness, and exhibits public responsibility
- Is responsive to a diverse environment
- Exhibits equity and fairness in all its dealings
- Maintains effective communications throughout its domain
- Cultivates a desire to belong

E. The Need for a Project Management Body of Knowledge

From the foregoing it will be observed that the relevant body of knowledge (PMBOK) is the cornerstone of PMI and its professional endeavors. A defined, published, and accepted body of knowledge reflecting good practice is essential as a guide to the development of a certification exam. It also serves to define what should be taught in a formal educational program, as well as serve as a set of criteria for evaluating such a program for accreditation purposes.

However, the world of project management is still developing and will continue to do so. Its range of applications is changing and spreading, and consequently, its practice continues to evolve. Therefore, any attempts to codify and document what is currently considered to be recommended good practice must also be permitted to evolve. Yet changes to the PMBOK must be developed with some care since the impact will be felt on the entire professional program of the Institute.

In short, the development of the PMBOK is a journey, not a destination. It is initially generic in nature, and its intent is to provide a common basis for understanding the process of project management across all areas of application, in all industries, and in all cultural regimes. It should cover all topics needed to understand and manage projects successfully.

F. Handbook Purpose and Content

This handbook is the first of a family of nine PMI educational handbooks dealing directly with the Project Management Body of Knowledge (PMBOK). It provides a general introduction to the subject and an overview and framework for all of the established functional areas of project management. It thus serves to introduce and to integrate the contents of the remaining handbooks, each of which deals with one of the functional areas. It is intended that the whole series cover essentially only that body of knowledge which constitutes "good generic project management practice," as reflected by its practitioners, and is appropriate for students of the PMP certification examination and similar or related PMI programs.

Consequently, these handbooks are not intended to cover the highly specialized expertise or advanced techniques of the supporting functions, for which other texts are available. They are intended to cover the *what* rather than the *how* of each of the identified project management functions. It is to be hoped that the contents of this handbook is a reasonable reflection of that intent.

These handbooks should be considered as *the first point of reference* for:

- Neophyte PM practitioners (those who want a summary of the basics of project management and references for more detailed information)
- Applicants for PMI's PMP certification program (i.e., those seeking the designation Project Management Professional)
- Short-course developers and trainers (and those seeking course recognition from PMI)
- Academics (those interested in areas for research or for accreditation of their degree programs by PMI)

This handbook is divided into four sections:

Part A looks at the management of projects from the outside and from a number of different viewpoints. This provides the reader with the basis for further reading and subsequent study.

Part B examines a number of common attributes of all project work, and discusses the requirements of a model intended to assist in a better understanding of project management. Such a model is proposed in Appendix A.

Part C deals with the uniquely dynamic nature of project management, principally as it affects, and is viewed by, those working from the inside of the process. It deals with the practical realities of a project and so is possibly the most challenging and of most immediate application. For example, a good project leader knows the right things to do, a good team knows how to do things right. To such a group project change is welcomed rather than feared, because the art of orientation and winning support is part and parcel of being an effective team player.

Part D, Conclusions, takes a brief look at the future of our rapidly developing profession.

For brevity and ease of reference, this handbook is deliberately structured to deal with its subject matter in simple and concise terms, often in bullet format or by graphic illustrations.

---

1. Abstracted from M. Barnes, Martin Barnes Project Management, UK, © 1988.
2. Abstracted from E. Jenett, About Project Management, *PM NETwork*, January 1991, p53.
3. D.I. Cleland, commentary to H. Padgham on "strategic issues" for PMI, December 7, 1990.
4. Dr. E. Obeng, Project Managers can Show the Way, *The Sunday Times*, November 18, 1990, Section 6.
5. Abstracted from T. Cooke-Davies, Return of the Project Managers, *Management Today*, BIM, UK, May 1990.
6. PMI-INTERNET Agreement dated October 16, 1990, p3.
7. A.S. Humphreys, Business Planning and Development, Inc., BIM (UK) Report, June 1986, p81.
8. D.I. Cleland, *Project Management: Strategic Design and Implementation*, Tab Books, Inc., PA, 1990, p53.
9. Studies conducted under the direction of Dr. John Adams, (then) PMI Director of Education, and presented to the PMI Board c. 1982, *Project Management Quarterly*, December 1982, p8; *Project Management Journal*, August 1986, p15; *PMBOK*, March 28, 1987, p0-1.
10. Minutes of Special Organizational Development Project meeting held January 27, 1989.

Chapter II   Definition and Content of Project and Program Management

A.   Project Definitions and PMI

The word *project* has come to be a household word in the English language. It has many meanings, but in particular is associated with a plan, scheme or undertaking for accomplishing a purpose. It is a method devised for attaining an end. It can therefore apply to *any assignment which will end when a goal is reached*. The essential point is that a project is not a permanent or long-term activity. Rather, it is any endeavor that ends with a specific, unique or infrequent accomplishment, end result, or product, which is its·distinguishing characteristic.

In practice, all projects have an unequivocal and formal goal orientation and a finite life cycle. That is to say, since a project is established to achieve a predetermined result, it has specific start and end points.[1] Also, the work to be accomplished is typically constrained by the limited availability of necessary resources. Therefore, PMI defines a project simply as:

Any undertaking with a defined starting point and defined objectives by which completion is identified. In practice, most projects depend on finite or limited resources by which the objectives are to be accomplished.[2]

It is a simple concept that can lead to a dramatically different management environment, as will be seen. It is the difference between maintaining the ongoing and creating something new! It is worth observing that this definition does not describe how the project objectives are to be achieved. This is reflected in PMI's definition of project management discussed in Section B.

Note that for PMI, discussion of projects is not limited to any particular field of activity such as construction. Nor is there any reference to size or duration. In fact, the PMI literature embraces all kinds of project work, in every field of project endeavor, in any location. Indeed, the tremendous diversity and worldwide membership of PMI, and the consequent exchange of ideas and experience, is PMI's strength.

Some people are involved in programs, or program management. While there is no universal consensus on definition, for PMI's purposes, programs are seen as a logical collection or series of related projects. In this sense, projects are a subset of programs. Therefore, the principles of project management are the same, although their application to programs may be significantly more complex.

B.   Project Management Definition

The resolution of a concise, comprehensive but defensible, generic definition of project management received regular attention in the PMI literature during the early years of the Institute. An appropriate definition gradually evolved from the original objectives of "on time and on budget" to the present-day definition. This definition not only recognizes four basic objectives, but also includes the more esoteric values which make a project successful. It also makes it clear that project management is both an art and a science involving pre-emptive integrated planning.

Thus, PMI defines project management as follows:

Project Management is the art of directing and coordinating human and material resources throughout the life of a project by using modern management techniques to achieve predetermined objectives of scope, quality, time and cost, and participant satisfaction.

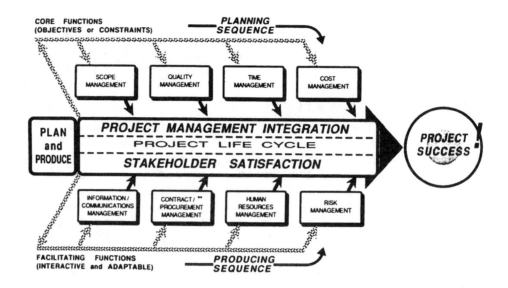

Figure II.1. Project Management Integration: The Source of Success

After Quaife, Jennett and others, c. October 1990

Figure II.1 provides a dynamic representation of the project management process. The four core management functions of scope, quality, time and cost, represent the project objectives (as in the view of the project sponsor) or constraints (as in the view of the project manager). However, the project is enabled by the four facilitating management functions of information/communications, contract/procurement, human resources, and risk. The two sets of functions are discussed in greater detail in Sections F and G below.

Project management integrates these functions progressively throughout the project life cycle, with the aim of satisfying the stakeholders according to the project's established requirements. Project success is typically generated when the stakeholders express their collective satisfaction.

The common underlying process is first to plan and then to produce. The arrows are intended to suggest an input/output system which, in many cases, is iterative, and, as discussed in Section H below, the priority sequence in planning tends to be clockwise through the diagram, while the producing sequence tends to be counterclockwise as shown.

C. Project Management is Unique (and Why)

Many have argued that managing a project simply requires the application of standard management principles to project-type work, that the body of knowledge is therefore the same and, consequently, there is no basis for an independent profession. Certainly there are similarities and overlaps. However, as noted in Section A, the very definition of project leads to a dramatically different management environment, so it is useful to compare an established ongoing enterprise with a project situation.

A well managed production or service organization is often characterized by:

- Roles and relationships are well-understood, having been developed and adjusted over lengthy periods;
- Tasks are generally continuous, repetitive or exhibit substantial similarity;
- Relatively large quantities of goods or services are produced per given time period;

- The workload tends to track external demand rather than special internal needs;
- Given these conditions, there is relative stability;
- Consequently, management of time is not a high priority;
- If change is minimal and protracted, it can be thoroughly programmed and progressively integrated; and
- Management concerns itself with projects only on an exception basis.

In summary, the work places of such enterprises are bounded by traditional hierarchies, lines of authority, centralized control and repetitive, assembly line-type jobs.

This is in marked contrast to the project environment which features:

- Temporary teamwork
- Informal relationships
- Complex management environment
- Specific time constraints
- Limited critical products
- Limited and/or shared resources
- Variable effort
- Measurable progress against plan
- Rapid change, and
- A satisfying conclusion.

Happily, for those inclined towards project work, this is a much more exciting and challenging work environment, even though a clear understanding of project management concepts is relatively new. However, associated with almost all projects are people who are not conversant with the process and who have their own priorities. This leads to stress and conflict, which needs special project management attention.

The project environment is discussed at greater length in Chapters V and VI.

D. Project Management is a Project-Oriented Process

If projects are defined in terms of specific objectives and constraints, then their achievement is a *process*. Therefore, it is important to recognize that when the term project management is used, it is the process, and not the (ongoing) management of the resulting product or facility which is being referred to. Indeed, project management is really a process of managing *people within a project-oriented environment*, and is certainly much more than just completing forms and counting hours against completed tasks.

Experience has shown that for project work the traditional management process breaks down and, consequently, new management philosophy, strategy and relationships are required. These tend to cut across the normal flow of corporate authority and responsibility and radiate beyond any single functional unit. In addition, the life cycle of the project management process has some very typical and distinctive but demanding characteristics, as will be seen from the next section.

E. The Project Time Frame

Successful project management requires careful planning to precede the accomplishment of the work itself. First planning and then producing is at the heart of the modern concept. Planning takes place in progressively more detail as the project progresses, but the project plan should be subjected to a critical review at a high level, prior to being finalized and approved for implementation. Thus, a major *go/no-go* decision point (or *Executive Control Point*, as discussed in Chapter VII.G), is established about midway through the total life of the project, as shown in Figure II.2.

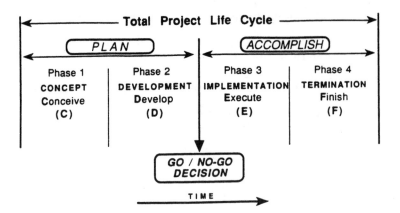

Figure II.2. Project Time Frame: Four Basic (Generic) Phases

The planning work preceding this executive control point is sometimes referred to as "upstream" or "soft" phases, while the production phases following the break point are referred to as "downstream" or "hard." In many project situations, crossing this boundary signals a major change in pace, change in the numbers and types of skills required, as well as in organizational structure. The work of the first two phases is typically reported or presented in a *Project Brief* (see Chapter VII.H), which provides the vehicle for formal approval and the agreed upon basis for the monitoring and control of the subsequent phases.

Through the work of contributors to PMI literature, it has been reasonably well established that a project typically passes through four distinct *project phases*. The two phases upstream may be referred to as *Concept* and *Development*, while the two downstream may be referred to as *Implementation* and *Termination*. Or they can be referred to as Conceive, Develop, Execute and Finish, which happens to be convenient because the sequence C, D, E, F, is easy to remember. In specific project applications other terms may be used respectively, such as Initiation; Planning, Feasibility or Definition; Execution, Installation or Construction; and Transfer, Product Shipped, Hand Over, or Commissioning.[3]

Collectively, these project phases are known as the *project life cycle*, and this project life cycle provides a major baseline for all practical, presentation and educational purposes. The Project Life Cycle is further explored in Chapter III.

F. The Four Core Functions[4]

The four functions of scope, quality, time and cost lead to specific objectives which are integrated with one another and with the project life cycle. Together they form the frame of reference for the project, against which the success of the project may be measured. From the sponsor's perspective, they represent a set of *requirements*; whereas, from the project manager's perspective, they represent *parameters*, or *constraints*. Either way, achieving these respective objectives or working within these parameters, constitutes the four basic project management functions.

The definition of the project's required products or outputs is known as the project's *scope*. Since the scope of a project must first be identified, developed, and then has the habit of changing during the rest of the project's life cycle, this gives rise to the need for *Scope Management*.

For the products of a project to be considered satisfactory, certain standards of *quality* must be defined and achieved. This leads to the need for *Quality Management*.

The life of a project is finite, which is to say that the time available for completion is limited. In reality, time itself is quite inflexible, but the activities required for the project must be carefully planned and scheduled if they are to be completed within the time available. This is referred to as *Time Management*.

"Time is money" is a well-recognized phrase in our society, so money is closely associated though somewhat more flexible. The consumption of resources to produce the project's scope also costs money, which therefore needs carefully managing under the heading of *Cost Management*.

G. The Four Facilitating Functions[5]

The four functions of risk, human resources, contract/procurement and information/ communications are the facilitating functions, because they are the means through which the objectives of the basic functions are achieved. They may be elaborated as follows.

As noted in the preface to this handbook, projects are launched for the purpose of implementing change. Even the process of project management itself is subject to a considerable amount of change during the course of its life cycle (see Chapter III.C). Because of the relative uniqueness of every project and the rapidly changing conditions referred to, the final outcome of every project is always *uncertain*.

Uncertainty is associated with *probability* and *risk*. Prudent management will take steps to *mitigate* the possibility that requirements will not be met, e.g.,by reducing the project risk wherever this can be achieved compatible with the overall project objectives. For this, a comprehensive understanding of the nature of the project is required at the outset, especially if it is complex and interdisciplinary. These activities are identified as *Risk Management*.

The reality is that projects are achieved through people and their respective skills and abilities. But the number of people and their types of skill varies considerably during the course of the project and, indeed, many are required on the project for only a short length of time. Normally, there will be a project team, led by a project manager, but even the project team is required only temporarily. Often these temporary alliances take place within a traditional management organizational setting, calling for an interactive and flexible relationship.

In this temporary setting, careful attention must be given to the assembly of people, their interactions and motivation to work together effectively through a clear understanding of their respective *roles and responsibilities*. This requires *Human Resources Management*.

People and their skills alone are not enough. It is the willing contribution of their services that is needed to execute the project. Services external to the organization may be purchased through an "arm's length" contract; that is to say, a formal, usually written arrangement vested in law. On many projects, materials and equipment must also be secured by contract.

The services of those within the organization, on the other hand, may have to be acquired through informal understandings. Indeed, people *negotiate* every day, with buyers, sellers, bosses, employees, people they work and associate with, in order to obtain formal and informal commitments. So it is a common experience that a major portion of a project manager's time must be spent in *procuring* peoples' *commitment to the project objectives, especially on in-house projects. Procurement, by the way, is the acquisition of something (anything) for money (or equivalent), including a job that pays wages, and includes carrying the obligation to a successful conclusion.*

Thus, the commitment of these goods and services to the project, as well as the administration of their conduct or delivery, are the responsibility of *Contract/Procurement Management*.

Sound project management requires developing a plan, collecting information on the *status* of the work at any given time, comparing it to the plan, and if necessary taking appropriate corrective action. But this only works if people know and understand the plan and any subsequent updates, and provide the necessary *feedback*. Often this feedback comes from sources both internal and external to the project, and can only be fully understood through a proper interpretation of the *project environment*. Responding to this environment is sometimes referred to as *public relations*.

Collectively, these activities come under the heading of *Information/Communications Management*.

H. Why the Function Sequence is Significant[6]

There is some degree of logic behind the sequence adopted for describing the current number of project management functions which may be helpful to the reader. It will be noted that this sequence is:

- Scope
- Quality
- Time
- Cost
- Risk
- Human Resources
- Contract/Procurement
- Information/Communications

Ordered in this way, the functions display a dynamic relationship which implies both a progressive flow of information as well as the flow of work through the project management process. The information flow represents WHAT is managed, while the process flow reflects HOW it is managed. Projects are planned by moving down the list, but are actively controlled by moving up the list.

Thus, projects are planned moving sequentially downward by examining:

- What needs to be done: SCOPE
- To what standards: QUALITY (specified)
- The time and sequential order of tasks: TIME
- How much the tasks/project will cost: COST
- What is the degree of certainty of the answer: RISK
- What is the quality of human performance required to achieve it: QUALITY (results)
- What kind of people are needed: HUMAN RESOURCES
- What commitments must be procured, or what resources must be contracted for: CONTRACT/PROCUREMENT
- How are all these people communicated with to get them to perform at the necessary level, to the quality of product needed, at the cost expected, and by the date required: INFORMATION/COMMUNICATIONS

In managing a project, on the other hand, the tendency is to move sequentially upward. First, communication must be effectively established with people to get them to do something, and refer to the contract or other form of commitment for the agreed upon details. The work is done by the type of people available or assigned, and this applies to the executives and line managers as well as members of the project team. They need to use their skills to move the project forward and, as noted above, the quality of their performance will determine the quality of the product regardless of the quality specifications.

In the planning process there is, of course, a great deal of iterating done, but the sequence does serve to provide linking and clarification. The first four functions are the traditional, well-defined passive components, which are usually documented and may be said to be *hard*, i.e., scope and quality by requirements and specifications, time by schedules and charts, and cost by budgets, reports and analyses. Time and cost are the harder by virtue of having a mathematical base. The last four, while documentable, require personal interaction and may be said to be the *soft* components of project management. They tend to be dependent upon the social sciences, by making a great deal of use of management theory.

Quality is a pivotal function because it bridges the transition between the hard and soft components since it has two parts, the hard part of product quality, and the soft part of the quality of human performance. It is the latter which in fact determines the quality of the product. The cost and timeliness of all these various activities required to produce the end products will together and in large measure determine the success of the project.

I. A Word About Work

PMI's current definition of *scope* encompasses both the products of a project, or component of a project, and the work content. It specifically comprises all activities performed, the resources consumed and the end products which result, including quality standards.[7] However, in a well-researched paper presented to the 1987 PMI Northwest Regional Symposium in Portland, Oregon, it states that "(This) concept...is unsatisfactory for management purposes. It is too broad, both because it incorporates the cost and schedule objectives and because it combines the planned work (means or methods) with the specification of required products (ends or goals)."[8]

For many, Schedule, Cost and Technical Performance form the three sides of a triangle (as shown on Figure A3.a, Appendix A). However, technical performance is now seen as the composite of two separate variables, Scope and Quality (see Chapter V.G), and the paper recommends that Scope must also be seen as distinct from work for effective management control. The paper defines Project Scope as "The bounded set of verifiable end products, or outputs which the project team undertakes to provide to the client (the owner or sponsor) of the project" or, more simply, "the required set of end results or products with specified physical and functional characteristics; the outputs."

This much tighter definition provides a clear standard against which the performance of the project process can be measured. This is because it differentiates between the constraint applied by the project sponsor and the work necessary to accomplish the project objectives, the means, methods, and management plans for which should be at the discretion of the project manager. While scope changes will still lead to changes in the work, it provides the means for distinguishing scope changes as the responsibility of the project sponsor from those changes in the work which may only be the responsibility of the project manager. Of course, any change in the work once approved or mandated by the project sponsor (for whatever reason, even though it does not change the end products) becomes a change to the contract between the parties.

The Portland paper goes on to say that "Achieving the right results, in other words, fulfilling the scope objective, is the primary test of effective performance by project management. It takes precedence over the constraints of deadlines and budgets. Failure to manage and control this aspect of the objectives (i.e., scope) is a principal reason why projects fail."

Work, on the other hand, is an integrator providing linkages between each of the project management functions, see Figure II.3. In this diagram:[9]

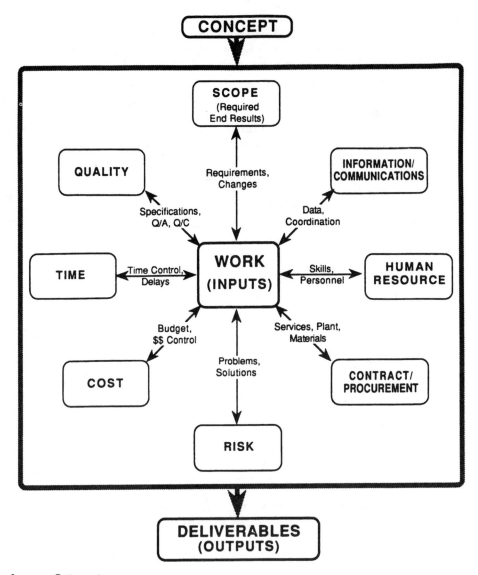

Figure II.3. Work as an Integrator

After C. Quaife © 1/11/91

- Scope determines the outputs that work must achieve during the project and each phase of it;
- Quality defines, assures and controls the quality standards of the work;
- Time plans, schedules and controls the progress of the work;
- Cost budgets, estimates and controls the cost of the work;
- Risk anticipates and controls the uncertainties involved in performing the work;
- Human Resources organizes and motivates the project team and others to do the work;
- Contracts (external and internal to the project team) defines who is to supervise and implement the work and administer the work contracted for; and
- Communications provides the necessary data for planning, coordinating and undertaking the work.

Drawing a clear distinction between scope and work, and developing a better understanding of each, is yet another example of the evolving nature of the project management body of knowledge.

1. M. Ahmed, D. Alderman, Project Management: A Management Accounting Perspective, The
    Society of Management Accountants of Canada, Hamilton, Ontario, 1986, p1 and 2.
2. *PMBOK*, March 28, 1987, p0-2.
3. Ibid., p1-2.
4. Ibid., p1-2.
5. Ibid., p1-3.
6. After letter from P. Nunn, *Project Management Journal*, August 1986, p105-108.
7. *PMBOK*, March 28, 1987, pA-5.
8. W.W. Wawruck, *Managing the Scope: A Neglected Dimension of Effective Performance on Diverse
    Projects*, PMI Northwest Regional Symposium, Portland, Oregon, 1987, p202.
9. C. Quaife, in private correspondence, January 1991.

Part B   Project Structure

Chapter III   The Project Life Cycle (plc)

A. The Life Cycle Definition and Hierarchy

As has been seen from Chapter II.E, the time frame for the project management process encompasses two sequential steps of planning and accomplishment. This subdivision was further divided into four distinct phases, which are typical of most areas of project application. They are therefore considered to be *generic*.

The project life cycle may be defined as:

The four sequential phases in time through which any project passes, namely: concept; development; implementation; and termination.

For practical purposes in the management of most projects, these four sequential generic phases need to be broken down into greater detail as shown in Figure III.1. That is, each phase may be made up of one or more stages and, for purposes of scheduling the actual work involved, each stage is further developed into a number of activities or tasks. These activities or tasks are obviously specific to the particular project. However it is interesting to note that the selection of appropriate stages is typically specific to the industry concerned, and only the principle of *plan and accomplish* and the next level of *four generic pahases* are applicable to projects generally.

Thus, from Figure III.1, Project Stages are subsets of Project Phases and hence project *phases* and *stages* may be defined as:

The division of a project time frame, or life cycle, into the largest logical collection of related activities. These phases may be further subdivided into stages appropriate to the project and its area of application.

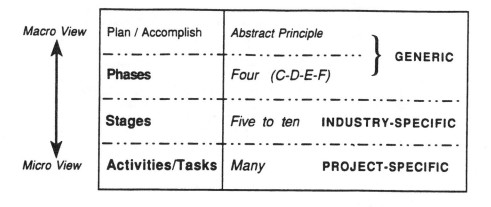

Figure III.1. The Anatomy of the Project Life Cycle

The relevance and consistency of the application of project management principles to all levels of the project life cycle from the macro to the micro is well worth noting. A specific task can just as well be considered as a "project" in its own right, and requires the same functional considerations, albeit on a lesser scale, as the project as a whole. It is rather like the well-known but extinct ammonite fossil which is coiled in a spiral, every section of which exhibits identical features but at ever decreasing scale. This phenomena is known to modern science as a fractal.[1]

Perhaps that is why breaking the project down into manageable work packages is so attractive. It enables the same standard approach to be applied throughout. It is also why some large projects seem to have multiple project managers.

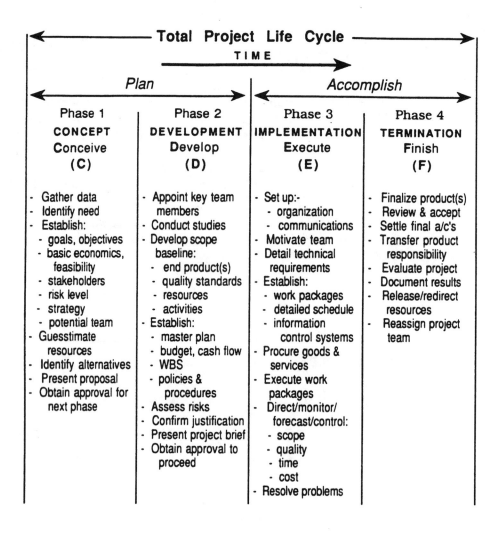

Figure III.2a.   Project Life Cycle: Stages/Activities
                   – Typical

B. Typical Project Phase Activities

Some typical project phase activities are shown in the following figures. Figure III.2a lists sets of activities applicable to most projects.[2] Figures III.2b, III.2c, III.2d and III.2e list the activities for construction,[3] manufacturing and distribution engineering,[4] new-product-introduction/information-processing-products,[5] and systems development,[6] respectively.

C. Some Distinctive PLC Variables

One of the distinctive characteristics of project management is the marked variation of some of its process features during the course of its life cycle. This is illustrated by the following curves:

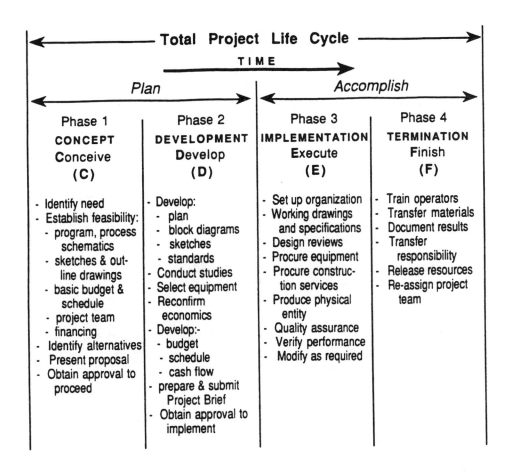

Figure III.2b   Project Life Cycle: Stages/Activities
– Construction

Level of Effort

To achieve any kind of output or product, an effort is required. But in the case of a project, the relationship between effort and time is quite distinctive. To visualize this relationship, consider a curve of effort plotted against time. Clearly, the effort starts at zero, before the project has commenced, and ends at zero, after it has been completed.

Between these two points, the effort-time curve has a typically characteristic profile. This may be likened to a pear sliced down the middle, one half of which rests flat face downwards, with the stem at time zero. The vertical profile is then representative of the project time-effort relationship. This profile, relative to the project phases discussed earlier, is shown in Figure III.3a.

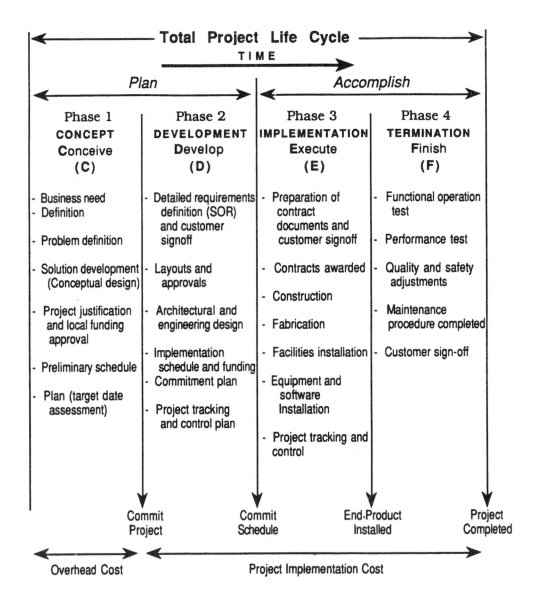

Figure III.2c. Project Life Cycle: Stages/Activities
– Manufacturing and Distribution Engineering

After L. A. Rogers, PMJ, August 1986, p109

The "S" Curve

The pear-shaped time-effort curve discussed in the previous subsection can also be plotted as a progressive cumulative total. In this case, it looks very much like an "S" with the bottom tail of the "S" at time zero, and the top tail corresponding to project completion at whatever time and effort is necessary to reach that point. Of course, the principle can be equally applied to any of the activities and tasks required as a component of the project and, as such, provides a powerful control tool. This technique is discussed in greater length in Chapter VII.F.

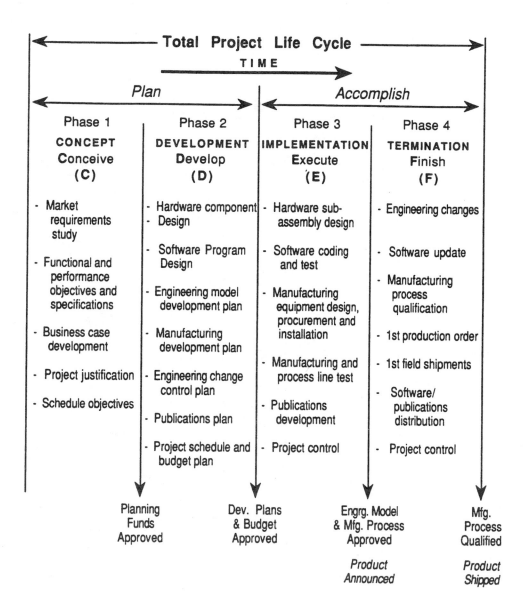

Figure III.2d.   Project Life Cycle: Stages/Activities
        – New Product Introduction and Information Products

After L. A. Rogers, PMJ, August 1986, p110

Potential for Adding Value

The potential for adding value to the products of a project are obviously highest during the formulation or concept phase, and lowest during the finishing phase. Between these two extremes, the curve tends to follow a reverse "S" curve as shown in Figure III.3b.

Escalating Cost to Change or Fix

The cost of making changes is lowest in the first two phases, but rises more and more steeply as the project progresses, as shown in Figure III.3c. In construction, for example, it has been suggested that the cost to make a change, or fix a non-conformance, increases by ten times in each succeeding phase.

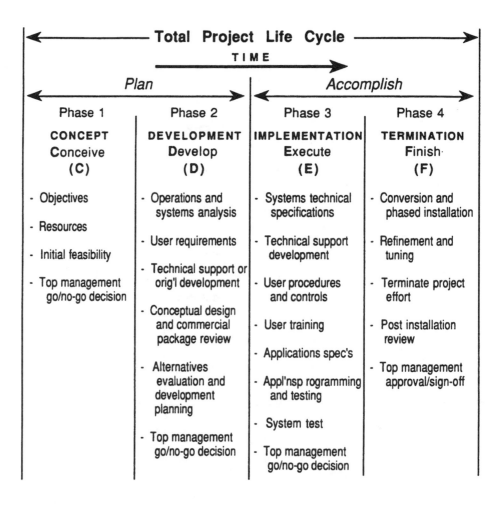

← Total Project Life Cycle →			
TIME →			
Plan		*Accomplish*	
Phase 1	Phase 2	Phase 3	Phase 4
CONCEPT Conceive **(C)**	**DEVELOPMENT** Develop **(D)**	**IMPLEMENTATION** Execute **(E)**	**TERMINATION** Finish· **(F)**
- Objectives - Resources - Initial feasibility - Top management go/no-go decision	- Operations and systems analysis - User requirements - Technical support or orig'l development - Conceptual design and commercial package review - Alternatives evaluation and development planning - Top management go/no-go decision	- Systems technical specifications - Technical support development - User procedures and controls - User training - Applications spec's - Appl'nsp rogramming and testing - System test - Top management go/no-go decision	- Conversion and phased installation - Refinement and tuning - Terminate project effort - Post installation review - Top management approval/sign-off

Figure III.2e.   Project Life Cycle: Stages/Activities
– Systems Development

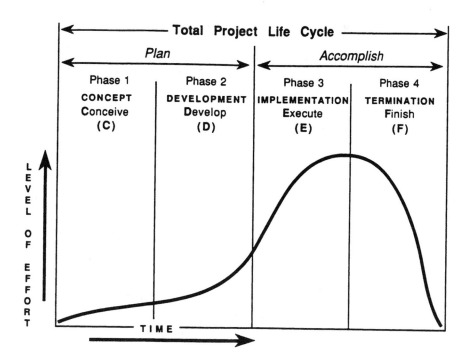

Figure III.3a. Typical Life Cycle Profile
　　　　　　– Level of Effort

Adding Value vs. Cost to Change

If the Cost-to-Change curve is superimposed over that of Adding-Value, the intersection probably represents the point at which a constructive opportunity changes into a destructive intervention, as shown in Figure III.3d.

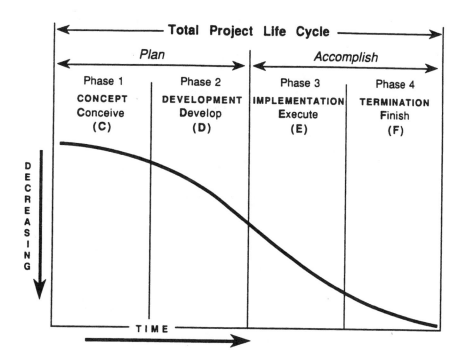

Figure III.3b. Typical Life Cycle Profile
　　　　　　– Potential for Adding Value

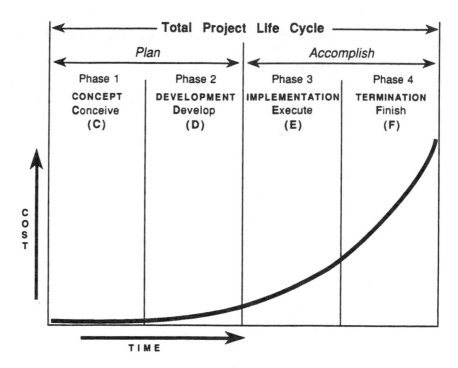

Figure III.3c. Typical Life Cycle Profile
– Escalating Cost to Change or Fix

Uncertainty vs. Amount at Stake

Comparing uncertainty or risk with the amount at stake, the level of uncertainty remains relatively high during the first two phases of the project and does not start to fall significantly until implementation progressively translates unknowns into knowns. The amount at stake, if measured in terms

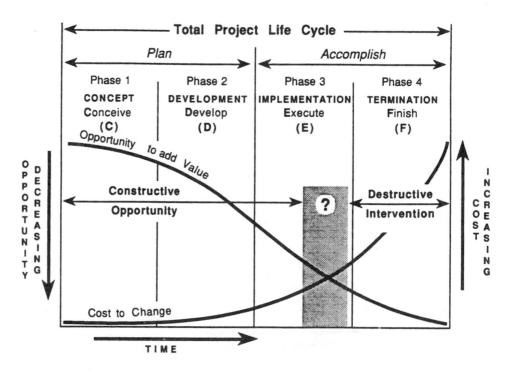

Figure III.3d. Typical Life Cycle Profile
– Adding Value versus Cost to Change

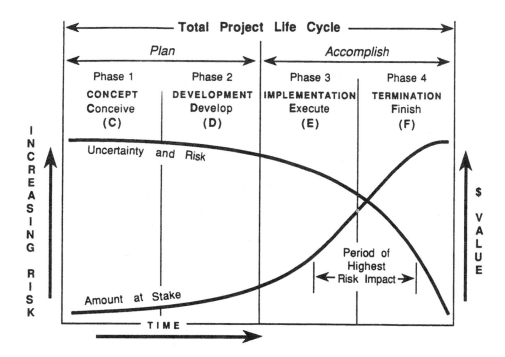

Figure III.3e. Typical Life Cycle Profile
– Risk versus Amount at Stake

of resources invested, on the other hand, is low during the first two phases, but rises rapidly during the execution phase. The factoring of these two variables on a particular project can lead to some very sophisticated analysis also involving probability. However, in simplistic terms, it may be deduced from Figure III.3e that the impact of risk is probably highest at the beginning of the finishing phase.

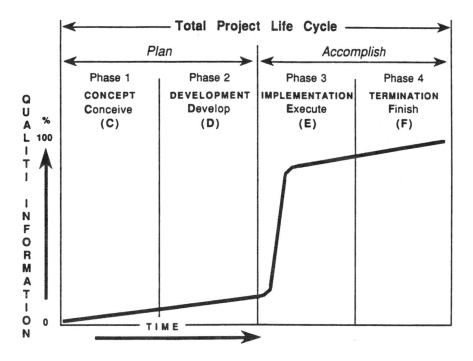

Figure III.3f. Typical Life Cycle Profile
– The Information Explosion

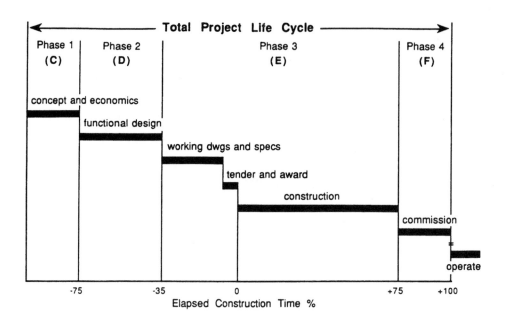

**Figure III.4a. Typical Project Bar Chart
  – Construction**

Information Explosion

The upstream phases of a project represent the development of information upon which the downstream realization phases can be based. However, the development of the large amount of data usually needed for the working details of execution are frequently planned as the first stage of that phase. For example, in construction projects, the preparation of working drawings and contract documents is usually the first stage of project implementation. Thus, there is a very rapid expansion of information at the beginning of the execution phase, as shown in Figure III.3f.

D. Project Stages are Industry-Specific

As illustration, several examples follow:

1. Construction – Figure III.4a shows a simple construction project bar chart.
2. Information Systems – Figure III.4b shows a simplified information systems project bar chart.
3. Defense System Acquisition – Figure III.4c shows a much simplified defense systems acquisition bar chart.

E. Corporate/Business and Facility/Product Life Cycles

It should be recognized that the project process is only a subsystem of a larger one, as shown in Figure III.5. In fact, a series of interrelated life cycles can be identified as shown in Figure III.6. Overall is the *corporate/business life cycle* which spans the time from policy planning, through identifying needs, to disposal of the facilities, products or services of the enterprise. The *facility/product life cycle* spans the life of specific facilities or products from feasibility to disposal.

By definition, the project life cycle spans only the period of bringing a particular facility, product or service into being. It is worth noting, however, that

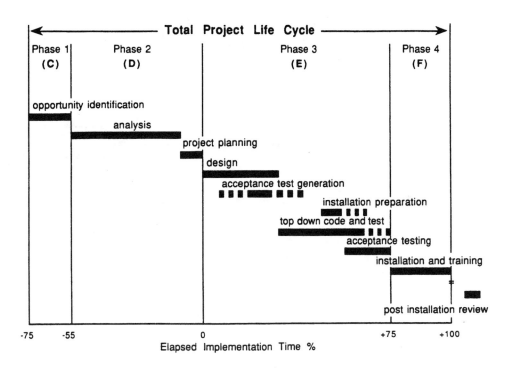

**Figure III.4b. Typical Project Bar Chart
– Information Systems**

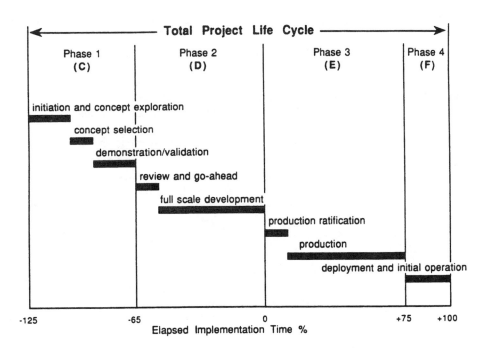

**Figure III.4c. Typical Project Bar Chart
– Defense Systems Acquisition**

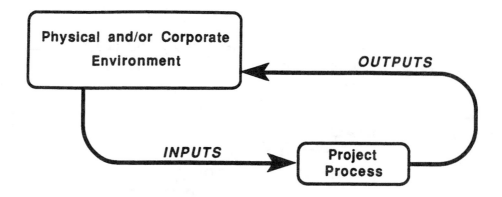

Figure III.5. A Project is a Subsystem of a Larger System

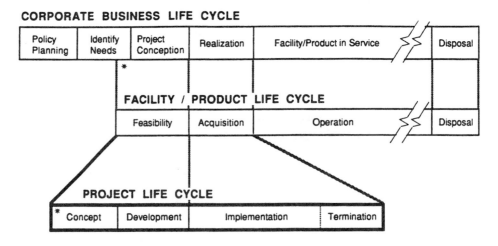

* Helping to identify the real needs in the project's
concept phase is vital to its eventual success.

**Figure III.6. Typical Project Life Cycle in the Context of
Corporate Business and Facility/Product Life Cycles**

the figure suggests that the project life cycle should start somewhat prior to the end of the Identify Needs phase of the Corporate Life Cycle. The ideal is to include a proper *needs determination* within the project process itself, as part of Concept formulation. Helping the corporation (or sponsor) to understand its needs is a vital part of understanding and developing the real project requirements, and hence a vital part of achieving eventual project success.

---

1. A "Fractal" is a series of self similar shapes of varying size. Every shape in the series is geometrically similar. Many obvious examples are found in nature such as the spiral shells of the common snail and many sea creatures. Less obvious examples include clouds, mountains, trees, river deltas, etc. The scroll casing of a water turbine is an engineering example. Fractals are used in mathematics to model complex natural processes.
2. *PMBOK*, March 28, 1987, p1-4.
3. R.M. Wideman, Cost Control of Capital Projects, AEW Services, 1983, p3.
4. L.A. Rogers, *Project Management Journal*, August 1986, p109.
5. Ibid., August 1986, p110.
6. R.M. Wideman, Lecture Presentation Notes, 1989.

Chapter IV   Modeling Project Management

A. The Role of Models[1]

The purpose of a model of the Project Management Body of Knowledge is to help to organize this knowledge so that it can be examined systematically and the scope of the profession evaluated accordingly. It also helps colleges and universities to structure programs for training project managers and for conducting research into project management. These tasks are formal parts of PMI's primary objective to advance the state-of-the-art in project management.

From the very start of PMI's ESA project (discussed in Appendix A) it was recognized that the purpose of project management is to achieve a number of concurrent major objectives by separate intellectual approaches, each of which breaks down into a number of topics and subtopics. Therefore, the ESA report was presented in the form of a set of work breakdown structures (WBS), to illustrate the relation and importance of the contents of each such subject area.

The WBS is very appealing in its simplicity, particularly to project managers who feel very comfortable with the WBS structure as a management tool. However, it is clear that the subject areas identified are themselves highly interrelated, and it is difficult to visualize the nature of these relationships. Thus, the Overview group at the 1985 Denver Symposium Special Workshop identified the need to review the WBS as a model to determine whether other models might be more applicable.

In fact, these relationships have since been the subject of considerable ongoing discussion, with a number of *graphic models* proposed to enhance understanding of the project management process, leading to a more useful organization of project management knowledge. There are no "right" or "wrong" models for this purpose, although there is no question that some models facilitate the organization of the knowledge better than others.

B. Model Requirements[2]

The purpose of a model or framework is firstly to organize and classify the body of knowledge and secondly to make certain that it is consistent. Thus, a sound structural PMBOK Framework is required for the purpose of "gluing it all together." To accomplish these goals, the model must:

1. Clarify the overall scope and extent of the comprehensive project management body of knowledge.
2. Break up the body of knowledge into logical and understandable categories or divisions.
3. Build on prior work.
4. Indicate the interrelationships between the various categories into which the PMBOK can be subdivided.
5. Take into account the complexities of project management and the integrating nature of the project manager's job and of his or her supporting team.
6. Provide a breakdown of the PMBOK into functions covering all subject areas of project management and their processes, activities, tools and techniques.
7. Be sufficiently simple and understandable to be useful (i.e., saleable) to present and potential project management practitioners.
8. Be consistent with the course content of PMI-sponsored project management education programs (at institutes of higher learning).

9. Be helpful to those organizations who should be managing by projects.

It should be emphasized that a framework or model, which describes the dimensions and components of the project management profession's body of knowledge, is a theoretical construct which can be comprehensive and all-inclusive. It may embrace new ideas and concepts from the academic side of the profession as well as new practices being tried out in the field. However, as with other professions such as law, medicine and accountancy, the "actual body of knowledge" rests with the practitioners and academics who apply and advance it.

Therefore, PMI's official PMBOK publications should encompass only those elements of the body of knowledge which, through application, have come to be generally accepted as "good" project management. That is, they should include only those elements of theory and practice whose use has become widespread enough to support a consensus about their value and usefulness.

For example, an article in a professional journal on a probabilistic method for analyzing the critical path (as opposed to the current, generally accepted deterministic method) is clearly a part of the project management profession's body of knowledge — it describes a technique for managing a project. However, until the new technique has proven useful in the field in a variety of situations, it will not be a part of PMI's generic PMBOK.[3]

C. PMBOK Boundaries[4]

The Denver Overview group recognized early in the discussion that there was a need to put limits or boundaries on the body of knowledge. It was also recognized that project management is a complex multidisciplinary profession which has considerable overlap into many other disciplines and professions. The degree of overlap is also greatly dependent upon which particular industrial sector, field or other application is using the project management approach. The three major points of overlap are in the areas of

1. General management
2. The technical area(s) in which the project is involved, and
3. The supporting or service areas which are also crucial to project success

This overlap can be depicted by a Venn diagram in which each circle represents a particular body of knowledge and the shaded areas represent the overlaps, as shown in Figure IV.1. How much overlap depends on the ground rules set to determine the scope of the PMBOK, and for this purpose it is worth examining the kinds of knowledge which are in the circles impacting project management.

D. Content of Related Bodies of Knowledge

General Management

While considerable controversy can be generated over what portions of the general (or business) management body of knowledge should be included in project management, there is usually little argument that the general management body of knowledge normally consists of:

*   Business Policy
*   Business Strategy
*   Planning and Controlling
*   Financial Management
*   Accounting
*   Business Economics
*   Information Systems
*   Organizational Behavior

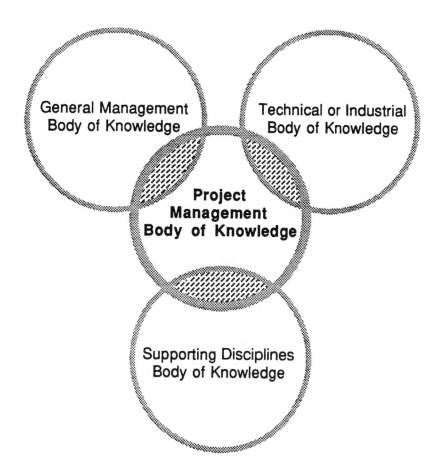

Note: Shaded areas show overlap with other bodies of knowledge.
Boundaries of knowledge are naturally fuzzy

Figure IV.1. Scope of the Project Management Body of Knowledge

PMBOK, March 28, 1987, p2-3

- Organizational Development
- Staffing
- Personnel Development
- Marketing and Sales
- Problem Solving
- Decision Making

Supporting Service Disciplines

Supporting or service disciplines are often essential for the success of project management, and parts of some of the following disciplines (or service functions) are included:

- Quality Assurance, Quality Control, Statistical Quality Control, etc.
- Configuration Management
- Logistics (Integrated Logistics Support)
- Contract Administration
- Procurement (Purchasing)
- Personnel Administration
- Facilities (Industrial) Engineering
- Legal
- Computer Programming

Technical/Industrial

The technical body of knowledge is somewhat more difficult to generalize since it is not truly represented by one circle in the Venn diagram. It really consists of a number of circles, each representing one of the industries, technologies, and professional areas in which project management is applied. Each has a large body of knowledge, much of which impacts in some manner on the project manager's job.

Indeed, project management is used in many types of industries or technologies, each of which may itself consist of different disciplines. Typical industries are listed in Appendix C3.

E. PMBOK Content Ground Rules

According to the Denver Overview group, from an examination of Figure IV.1, the following ground rules are appropriate for scoping the project management body of knowledge:

1. Much of the general management body of knowledge should be recognized as a given or prerequisite for project management and not included in the PMBOK unless aspects of this knowledge are an integral part of the project management process.
2. The PMBOK should not include major areas of other disciplines, professions or detailed knowledge particular to a specific industry unless this information is also an integral part of the project management process.
3. The PMBOK should not contain knowledge, technology, techniques or skills which are primarily limited to one industry or technology. That is, all items should have broad appeal in almost every area of project management application.
4. The PMBOK should not include major portions of supporting or service disciplines unless they are generally applicable to most projects. Such disciplines stand on their own and are principally utilized as tools of project management. Only those specific applications which reinforce the job of the project management team should become part of the PMBOK.
5. The PMBOK should emphasize knowledge, skills and techniques which are either unique to project management, or are fundamental to carrying out the project management process.
6. There is a definite need for the overlaps in the various bodies of knowledge as indicated in Figure IV.1. Project managers and their teams have a thorough grasp of project management, some expertise in general management and a good understanding of the particular project field.

The currently included functions of project management are shown in Figure II.1.

F. PMBOK Function Content

For convenience of reference, the contents of each of the functions is represented and coded according to a work breakdown chart. The official structure and content of the complete PMBOK is set out in a formal PMBOK document issued by the Project Management Institute, as approved by its Board of Directors from time to time. It is available from PMI's Central Administration Office. The potential structure and content of a typical project management function is discussed more fully in Appendix B.

---

1. *PMBOK*, March 28, 1987, pp2-1, 3-1, 3-2.
2. Ibid., p2-3.
3. Abstracted from correspondence by W. Duncan, PMI member, © September 1990.
4. *PMBOK*, March 28, 1987, p2-2.

Part C   Project Dynamics

Chapter V   Project Environment I - Internal Interfaces

A. Who is Really in Charge?

From the very generalized definition of a project discussed in Chapter II.A, it is clear that projects come in all shapes and sizes, and undoubtedly the internal environment varies in each accordingly. This environment is generally reflected in answers to the questions: what, where, when, why, who, how, and how much, and is perhaps best illustrated by the integrative PMBOK Framework model proposed in Appendix A. The project environment also gives rise to a need for such management sciences as psychology, organizational behavior and interpersonal communications, if the project is to be prosecuted successfully!

A leading question often asked is: "Who is really in charge—owner, sponsor, financier, the corporate organization and its governing body, or its political masters, client, project manager...?" The potential list is lengthy, and the particular labels used vary with the type of project. Whatever the answer, it is also important to understand the respective roles of the various parties, and the continuous breakdown of project *authority, responsibility* and *accountability* in particular.

Typically, the party that needs the change resulting from the project, and who will be its custodian on completion, is the *Owner*. The party that identified the need, and probably its leading protagonist, is the project's *Sponsor*, who may or may not be the same as the owner. If the project is being financed by other than the owner directly, this is usually achieved through some formal financial arrangement independent of the project, in which case the *Financier's* role is that only of holding a watching brief over the project's development and progress in order to protect his or her interests.

If the sponsor is a corporate body, that body should appoint a *Project Director* as their individual representative. This is in order to provide singular owner/sponsor *direction* for the project, and through whom proper *authority, responsibility* and *accountability* must flow to the party *managing* the project, namely, the *Project Manager*. Failure to do this will inevitably lead to less than satisfactory results, and as has been experienced on some unfortunate projects, may even compromise safety. The source of the project director's authority, especially if it is a collective body, is sometimes referred to as the *Executive Authority*.

It will be seen that the project manager is acting in a *service* role, and so the sponsor is the project manager's *client*. It is the project manager's job to take whatever authority, responsibility and accountability is delegated (the three must go together for effective management) and in turn delegate them fully, consistently and completely for the proper functioning of the project management process. This distribution is usually achieved through some form of work breakdown structure.

For those under "contract" to the project manager, or at least under his or her direction, the project manager is their "client" or "boss," and so on, down the chain. Conversely, to the project manager, those under "contract" may be vendors, contractors, or just simply regular employees. So one's view of the project, and corresponding terminology, depends very much on where one is in the overall scheme of things.

For purposes of this handbook, the source of the project manager's authority will simply be referred to as the *Sponsor*.

B. The Project Manager's Role

It has been suggested that the single common trait to be found amongst successful project managers is "an obsession with getting things done."[1] However, professional skill and ability must be applied by project managers and their teams in managing the resources and processes required if useful end results are to be successfully achieved from a concept or idea.[2] Therefore, in a well-organized project, the project manager must be vested accordingly with authority and responsibility. With this comes a certain status which facilitates interpersonal relations and access to information. It is this information which enables the project manager to develop strategies for the project team and to make and/or delegate decisions. Thus the project manager's role may be elaborated as follows:[3]

Interpersonal

As a figurehead, the project manager performs some ceremonial duties on the project. But this is part of the leadership role, which ideally should also include hiring and training staff, motivating, counseling, matching staffing needs with project functional requirements, and managing conflict. The influence of the project manager is most clearly seen in this leadership role, which also extends beyond project bounds to influence the organization's chain of command and outside contacts.

Informational

A well-organized project Information/Communications function will ensure that the project manager will receive quality information from subordinates as well as from outside sources, and thereby develop a powerful data base of relevant information. This data base is usually augmented by personal observation and, as well, by receiving and processing unsolicited information. The project manager thus becomes a nerve center for the project organization, and by disseminating privileged information to peers and subordinates is able to exercise considerable influence over the project process. The project manager also acts as the spokesperson in conveying information outside the project group, and in informing and influencing the decisions of the top management who have organizational control over the project.

Decisional

Information, experience and courage to decide with incomplete data, provides the input to decision making. As the project team's decision maker, the project manager may be acting as:

a. Interpreter and communicator of project priorities
b. Resource allocator, deciding who will get what priorities
c. Monitor, on the look out for new ideas
d. Entrepreneur seeking ways to improve group performance in a changing environment

By exercising these powers, project managers ensure that decisions are interrelated and also retain the power of reviewing and authorizing important decisions before they are implemented.

C. Organizational Power Structure[4]

The technological and behavioral changes that are shaping the nature of work today necessitate that project managers develop a better grasp of issues relating to organizational leadership, power and influence. With this awareness, they may avoid being overwhelmed by the pathological aspects of modern organizations, e.g., the bureaucratic infighting, parochial politics, destructive power struggles and the like, which reduce initiative, innovation, morale and professional excellence. As examples, an understanding of the Human/Resources function will facilitate:

Improving Personal Effectiveness

Project managers typically depend on diverse groups of professional and technical people (support staff and peers) over whom they may have little direct formal control. Therefore, it is imperative that they consider work in more relational terms, and recognize organizational power and leadership issues. They need to cut through the web of interdependent relationships and work with a diverse group of staff, who, themselves, may be operating under conflicting demands and priorities. Satisfactory progress requires systematic attention to these relationships, and to issues of cooperation and resistance as it affects the project.

Developing Adequate Power Base

Project managers need to use their power and influence appropriately to make up for the power gaps which are inherent in their positions. By establishing a powerful information base, as suggested in Chapter V.B above, developing critical cooperative relationships, expanding personal skills, they may gain control of important resources and thereby establish a strong track record. Project managers who are successful in developing such qualities emerge as effective leaders in the organization.

Influence/Cooperation Beyond Formal Authority

In technical and professional positions, there exist power gaps associated with relationships outside of the formal chain of command. This situation is often complicated by other factors which include lateral job relationships, diversity of locations, differences in goals, priorities and beliefs of the project participants, as well as ambiguity in their roles. Project managers need to identify such factors, assess who resist cooperation and why, and design incentives to maximize cooperation by project participants for the overall good of the project.

D. Influencing the Project's Cultural Environment[5]

The manager of the successful project will recognize the need to spend some effort in influencing the project's cultural environment for the benefit of the project stakeholders. Every project team member, indeed every member of the workforce, needs to be persuaded to convey the attitude *We care!*

Every decision and action should be designed with a view to making the stakeholder's experience better than it would have been had the project not been implemented. Therefore, the project management focus needs to be more on the quality of the stakeholder's experience at every stage of the project than on an overriding preoccupation with computer printouts and weekly progress reports.

The project's executive should also recognize, at the outset of the project, the important contribution that project management training can make to improving the project's cultural environment. Such training provides a powerful tool in developing competency and commitment to the project, in improving team performance, and ultimately, in final project quality.

E. Effective Internal Strategies[6]

Practical experience has identified a number of prerequisites which enable project management success. While these prerequisites do not necessarily guarantee success of future projects, their absence may well lead to sub-optimal results, if not outright failure. The Executive responsible therefore has a vital role to play by insisting on the following:

Executive support. The Executive must clearly demonstrate support for the project management concept by active sponsorship and control.

External authority. The project manager must be seen as the authoritative agent in dealing with all parties, and be the single formal contact with them.

Internal authority. The project manager must have the necessary managerial authority within his own organization to ensure response to his requirements.

Commitment authority. The project manager must have both the responsibility and authority to control the commitment of resources, including funds, within prescribed limits. The results of these decisions must be both accountable and visible.

Involvement in all major decisions. No major technical, cost, schedule, or performance decisions should be permitted without the project manager's participation.

Competence. The project manager and his supporting team members must be competent. Other functional personnel assigned to the project must also be competent.

Project team. The project manager should have a say in the assembly of the project team, to assure competence and help in obtaining their personal commitment, support and required quality of service.

Management information system. An effective project-oriented information and control system must be in place.

F.   S, Q, T, & C: Combinations and Relationships

The four management functions covering the four basic project objectives of scope, quality, time and cost were identified in Chapter II.B and described in Chapter II.F. These objectives provide the basis for determining the measures by which the success of the project can be assured. However, as every project manager knows from experience, these objectives, or constraints, are very much intertwined, and are not necessarily mutually compatible. Indeed, many of the project manager's decisions may have to be based on what is an acceptable trade-off between all four.

Interestingly, combinations of these objectives also have significance in terms of the product of the project reaching the marketplace. This is shown dramatically in Figure V.1.[7] The combination of scope and cost determine the product viability. The combination of cost and time represents the effort required or the use of resources in the process, while scope and quality together represent technical performance of the product. The combination of time and quality of the product, as well as cost, determines to a large degree whether or not the product is acceptable at a time when it is needed, i.e., whether or not it is competitive.

Such combinations are significant measures of internal project success.

G. The Tetrad Trade-off: Varies with Type of Project

As has been seen earlier, project management seeks to achieve its objectives, as defined by the parameters of scope, quality, time and cost, with the overall perception of the project as being satisfactory, and hence successful. In practice, however, project circumstances often prevail wherein the objectives relative to each constraint may not all be feasible or compatible. This is especially true when considerations of risk and uncertainty come into play.

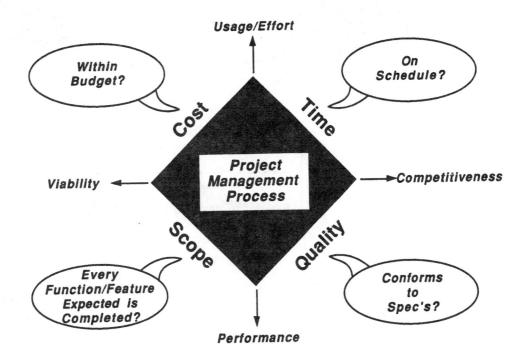

Figure V.1. Market's View of Project Management
After W. S. Ruggles & Associates, Inc., Training Course, Section 2, p.1, © 1989

More particularly, some projects may lean more towards one constraint than another. Therefore, the project manager and his team, in the course of managing the project process, must choose options and make decisions according to such priorities. This may be viewed graphically as the Tetrad Trade-off, as shown in Figure V.2.

In this diagram, four projects are shown, one in each of the four quadrants of the tetrad. The projects have "handles" which are intended to represent vectors signifying the extent and bias of (or pull on) the particular project as a consequence of the four constraints. Thus, project P_1 is in the scope emphasis quadrant and its priority leans towards defining the project scope (rather than developing a defined scope). Good examples include research and development (R & D) and defense projects. Such projects consequently tend to be very uncertain in terms of quality, time and cost.

More often, the scope is reasonably well defined, but the emphasis may be on quality, as represented by P_2. Examples include new high-end-market automobiles, high-end residential or commercial office construction, or heavy-duty public infra-structure projects, where durability and public safety are key concerns. Conversely, P_3 is in the time emphasis quadrant, as in the case of meeting the opening day deadline of a national exposition, or the opening night of a theater production. Or the emphasis may be on a balance between scope and cost, P_4, such as in the case of market research projects, or in some government studies.

The inexperienced project manager should be cautioned that the priority emphasis for a project may well shift during its life cycle. For example: a scope- and quality-oriented project at the outset may well shift towards cost and schedule towards the end of its life cycle. An illustration of this might be a project which, having experienced cost overruns, is running out of financing.

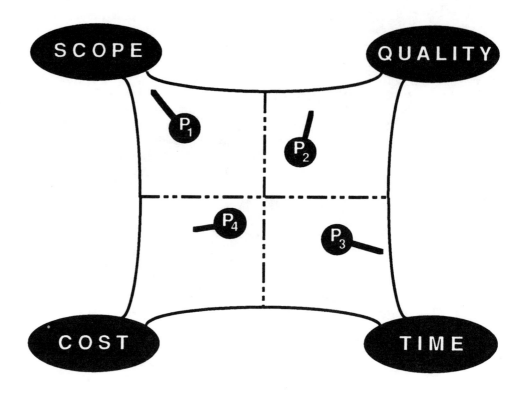

Figure V.2. The Tetrad Trade-off: Emphasis Varies with Type of Project and Often with Project Phase

Conversely, a cost- and schedule-oriented project may have a tendency to move towards scope and quality towards its end. An illustration of this might be a product launch which needs to be moved "up-market" as a result of new market competition. However, this latter shift is difficult to achieve in retrospect, and emphasizes the importance of sound early project planning and development.

Managing the Tetrad Trade-off with skill and understanding is a very important part of managing a project. Rarely does a project manager have the luxury of a project which has equally balanced constraints, such that the achievement of all four is entirely feasible!

H.   R, H/R, C/P, & Info/Comms: Integrative Function Relationships

In a somewhat similar way, the integrative functions are also interrelated, as shown in Figure A.10. In the figure for example, scope and cost are shown as having a significant tie to risk. Scope was discussed in Chapter II.F, and may be considered effectively described when end-products (together with quality requirements) are fully defined such that the work of project implementation can be competently scheduled and estimated. Of course, in real life, rarely is it possible to fully describe the scope of a project at the outset. This simply means an increase in the project risk. The less effective the scope definition, the greater the project risk.

Effectiveness of the overall project process in all likelihood is a combination of the management of human resources, information/communications, contract/procurement, plus effective planning and control.

However, these various relationships are not well understood, and will benefit from further research.

I. Relationship Between the Core and Facilitating Functions

As discussed in Chapter II.H, the four Core Functions of project management reflect the objectives of the project, or the *what* of "what is to be achieved." In contrast, the Facilitating Functions provide the means for accomplishing these objectives, or the *how* in "how it is to be achieved." The process of project management is the integration of these two types of functions, which leads to the ultimate goal of project success, as depicted in Figure II.1, Chapter II

The Core Functions tend to make use of mathematics, as in scheduling or cost control, or mathematical precision, as in specifying, dimensioning, or statistical quality control. In contrast, as noted in Chapter II.H, the Facilitating Functions require positive interaction between people, and therefore depend much more on management theory in the social sciences.

---

1. A. Stretton, in discussions, January 17, 1991.
2. PMI-INTERNET Agreement dated October 16, 1990, p3.
3. S. Zuberi contributed in a letter dated June 5, 1990.
4. Ibid., 1990.
5. R.M. Wideman, Managing the Project Environment, Dimensions of Project Management, H. Rescke and H. Schelle (Eds), Springer-Verlag, Berlin, published in honor of Roland Gutsch, © 1990.
6. Ibid.
7. After W.S. Ruggles & Associates, Inc., training course graphic, Section 2, p1, © 1989.

Chapter VI   Project Environment II - External Interfaces

A. What is the Project External Environment?

As important to a project's eventual outcome as the controlling of events within the project organization are its linkages to its external environment, frequently more so. The project manager's job is therefore not confined just to internal considerations, it must also be outward looking.

The project's external environment includes virtually everything outside the project: its technology (the knowledge base it must draw from); the nature of its products; customers and competitors; its geographical setting; the economic, political and even meteorological climate in which it must operate, other projects, and so on. Some of these factors are depicted graphically in Figure VI.1. All these factors, but particularly *changes* in them, can significantly affect the project process and its consequent success.

Figure VI.1. Project Environment: External Influences and Interfaces

Generally, the more a project is dependent upon the external environment, the greater the degree of uncertainty. However, the extent and mix of linkages will certainly vary from project to project. The purpose in analyzing them is to define potential problems, to assess the probability of their occurrence, and to try to solve them ahead of time. These issues should largely be addressed within the project management function of *Risk Management*.

B. Some Typical External Influences

Since the project manager and his team must be constantly aware of external influences, which may impact the progress and ultimate success of the project, some typical examples follow:

Sponsor expectations. Ensuring that the specified project objectives are in fact congruent with the real project needs, as indicated in Chapter III.E, is an important prerequisite during the upstream project planning. Further, it is important that this is monitored for change as cautioned in Chapter V.G. This is especially necessary if the sponsor is represented by more than one group with differing perspectives within the sponsor's own organization.

Financial/economic conditions. The viability on which the success of the project was predicated may change during the life of the project and, consequently, require modification of objectives. Examples: increase in interest rates, or fall in economic activity.

Technological/industrial conditions. May impact the progress and effectiveness of the project process. Example: appearance of a competitor's technological breakthrough.

Parent organization. The effects of the organization's standards, such as Policies and Procedures, may impact the conduct of the project. Example: revision of corporate policy.

Legal and regulatory requirements. Will impact any goods and services contracted for externally "at arm's length," as well as the conduct of internal activities. Example: stiffening of codes in response to environmental pressures.

Political implications. May be indirect and more obscure but can have a major impact, especially on infrastructure-type projects. Example: change of government at any level.

Health and safety standards. Must be observed, and if well maintained, can have a very favorable effect on project morale, progress and quality. Example: the results of workforce training.

Natural environment protection. Recognition that natural resources are finite, and must be protected and conserved, is an important consideration in the ultimate acceptability of infrastructure-type projects. Example: other concurrent projects may together overload the natural environment.

Changing workforce.[1] The workforce mix in terms of women, minorities and immigrants is changing in many parts of the world. It is becoming better educated and versed in today's technologies, and is moving from manual and clerical to knowledge skills. Example: changes in the perception of acceptable working conditions.

Social responsibilities.[2] Recognition of shifting needs such as reducing risk, providing interesting work, a healthier environment and improved opportunities. Example: shifting perceptions may result in loss of stakeholder interest in the project.

Ethical issues.[3] Hidden information and agenda are no longer acceptable to today's information-conscious public. Honesty and integrity are therefore of prime importance to the success of a project and to an ability to stand the scrutiny of both peers and society once the project is completed. Example:

exposure of unacceptable practices on other similar projects may heighten awareness of these issues.

Project management knowledge. Is expanding like any other discipline, and project managers have a duty to remain current in both the art and science. Example: better understanding of the mechanics of each of the project management functions.

C. The Environment from the Project Perspective

Since the project environment described in Section A is all-encompassing, and theoretically extends to infinity, ways and means are necessary for visualizing specific elements. The impact of the environment on a project is shown simplistically in Figure VI.2, and some suggested environmental groupings are shown in Figure VI.3.[4]

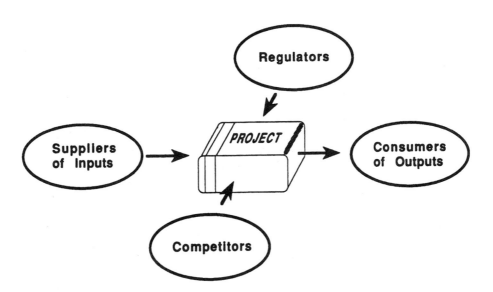

Figure VI.2. Project Environment Process

After N. R. Burnett and R. Youker, EDI Training Course CN-848, July 1980.

D. Developing Effective External Strategies[5]

Just as the means of influencing the project's internal cultural environment, as described in Chapter V.D, was one of developing the right attitude, so it is with developing a sound external stakeholder environment. Perhaps this attitude is best reflected by adopting a mind set that reverses the traditional organization chart hierarchy. In other words, place the project stakeholders at the top of the chart, followed by the front-line project team members, and on down to the project manager at the bottom. Perhaps the project team will then better visualize their truly service orientation, designed to serve the best interests of a successful project outcome, both perceived and in reality.

Steps In the Process

a. Learn how to identify and understand the role of the various stakeholders, how this information may be used as an opportunity to improve both the

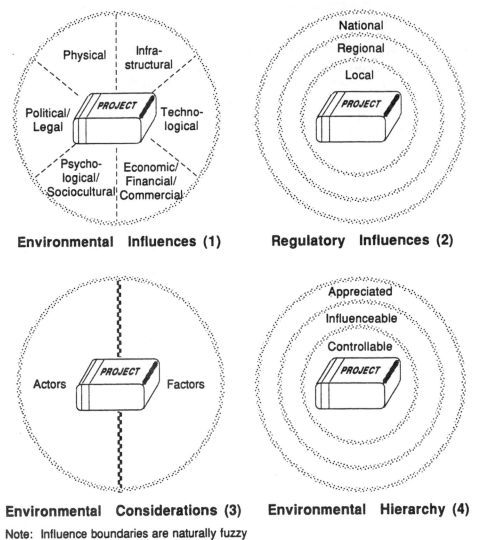

Environmental Influences (1)   Regulatory Influences (2)

Environmental Considerations (3)   Environmental Hierarchy (4)

Note: Influence boundaries are naturally fuzzy

Figure VI.3. Project Environment Influences
After N. R. Burnett and R. Youker, EDI Training Course CN-848, July 1980.

perception and reception of the project, as well as in developing the project scope definition.

b. Identify the real nature of each stakeholder group's business and their consequent interest in the project.

c. Understand their behavior and motivation.

d. Assess how they may react to various approaches.

e. Pinpoint the characteristics of the stakeholders' environment and develop appropriate responses to facilitate a good relationship.

f. Learn project management's role in responding to stakeholders' motives.

g. Determine the key areas which will have the most impact on the successful reception of the project.

h. Develop a Project Acceptance Plan aimed at managing/meeting external stakeholders' interests.

Remember always that even a minor stakeholder group may discover a "fatal flaw" in the project plan which could bring it to a standstill!

Identifying and Classifying the Stakeholders

One technique for dealing effectively with the project's external environment is to prioritize the various stakeholder linkages by conducting a *stakeholder analysis*. Such an analysis would be designed first to identify all the potential stakeholders who might have an impact on the project, and then to determine their relatively ability to influence it.

Stakeholders may be found in any of the following groupings:

a.   Those who are directly related to the project: for example, suppliers of inputs; consumers of outputs; and all those involved in the project process itself;
b.   Those who have influence over the physical, infrastructural, technological, commercial/financial/socio-economic, or political/legal conditions;
c.   Those who have a hierarchical relationship to the project such as government authorities at local, regional and national levels; and
d.   Those individuals, groups and associations, who have vested interests, sometimes quite unrelated to the project, but who see it as an opportunity to pursue their own ends, such as competitors and special interest groups.

Having identified the various stakeholders, each may be assigned to a category according to their relative ability to influence the project. Three possible categories include:

a.   Those whose requirements can be moderated or constrained,
b.   Those whose requirements can be influenced, and
c.   Those who need to be appreciated.

Within each of these categories, the stakeholders may be further rated by degree of significance according to their ability to influence the project outcome. Appropriate members of the project team can then prioritize their efforts accordingly, to maintain healthy linkages designed to provide the greatest probability of ultimate project success.

Influence by Project Public Relations

If the project is sufficiently large or important, the interface with much of the external environment may be assigned to a specific group within the project team.

Traditional management has long since recognized the classic Input-Process-Output model with its management feedback loop for process control, as discussed in Chapter VII.C. Dynamic managers also recognize that opening communication channels in both directions constitutes a powerful motivator at the operative level. Whether quality information is presented in verbal, written or graphical form, improvement in performance can be quite remarkable. Indeed, many knowledge-workers demand it.

This principle is just as true in the field of projects, though regretfully somewhat less evident. Nevertheless, on a major project, especially if it is publicly funded, providing a general information center is quite common. A more pro-active stance, or positive feed forward, as shown in Figure VI.4, is usually known as *public relations*, or just PR, and becomes a vital part of improving the understanding and perception, and hence reception, of the project

To a surprisingly large extent, the project team's ability to exercise this positive feed forward will determine their ability to control the project in terms of its final cost and schedule.

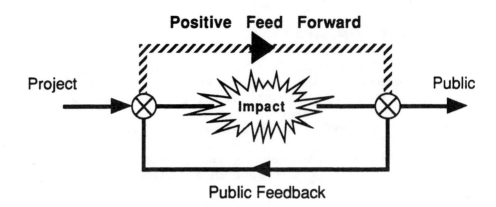

Figure VI.4. Managing the Environment: The Public Relations Concept

E. Public Relations Program Summary

The strategies discussed above may be briefly summarized as follows:

- Recognize the need to interface with the project's publics (both internal and external);
- Establish a positive "PR" philosophy;
- Identify the target audiences;
- Develop a "Model PR Program" designed to improve the project's environments;
- Develop a work breakdown structure for the PR program;
- Implement and monitor the plan;
- Run it like a subproject; and
- Enjoy a successful master project!

---

1. S. Zuberi contributed in a letter dated June 5, 1990.
2. Ibid.
3. Ibid.
4. R. Youker, *Analyzing the Project Environment, 13th Asian Development Bank Seminar MS, Manilla, Philippines, 1987.*
5. R.M. Wideman, *Dimensions of Project Management* Chapter: Managing the Project Environment, Springer-Veriag, New York, 1990.

Chapter VII   Project-Oriented Controls

A. Purpose - To Keep on Track

From time to time, there is a lot of discussion as to whether project management is really an art or a science. Those who specialize in applying the latest tools and techniques to their project work often see it as strictly scientific. For example, in the project context, PMBOK defines *management* systematically as *the process of planning, organizing, executing, coordinating, monitoring, forecasting and exercising control*,[1] where *control* is defined as *the exercise of corrective action as necessary to yield a required outcome consequent upon monitoring performance.*[2] However, as many practicing project managers have observed, what actually happens on a project seems to be anything but scientific. So there seems to be some confusion.

When it comes to talking about how control should be exercised on, or over, a project, there seems to be even more confusion. The fact is, the standard corporate management approach of work authorization and record keeping, financial reporting on a fiscal basis, payment authorization and accrual accounting, is simply not adequate for project work. This is because these are essentially historical perspectives, even though little can be done to change the past.

In contrast, projects are established to make changes for the future, a future which can be influenced. For this purpose, project-oriented controls are required in which baseline plans and budgets are established, progress and incurred costs are recorded on a project-to-date basis, and forecasts are regularly prepared which maintain a constant focus on this future. So the focus of project management is in the future direction. Not just any direction, of course, but specifically towards the predetermined project goals.

The project management process might be likened to driving an automobile. First and foremost is to have a sense of direction, where we want to get to. Then comes a road map, and a set of directions as to how to get there. To get there as soon as possible, we select the best route, and steer accordingly. What we are doing when we are driving is regularly checking road conditions and

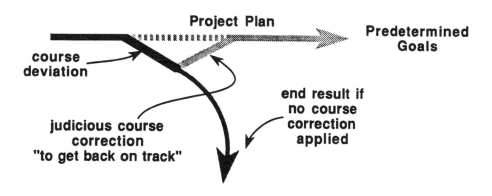

Figure VII.1. Keeping on Track

direction, and making appropriate course corrections. The same should be true of managing a project. Figure VII.1 illustrates the concept, and further suggests that, rather than major course corrections, smoother (optimum) performance can best be achieved by a series of "gentle nudges."

B. POETS can be Helpful

Perhaps the best way of remembering this plan-check-correct cycle is by adopting the mnemonic *POETS*, standing for *Plan, Organize, Execute, Track and Steer!* as shown in Figure VII.2. Each component of this process is more particularly described as follows:

Plan

The first step in any project is to plan the project with respect to scope, quality, time and cost. What precisely is to be achieved? Why? What is the process and purpose involved in the end product? How is the job to be done? Why should the project be done one way rather than another? Indeed, why should it be done at all? Where is it to take place? Who will design and implement it? What resources in terms of manpower, materials financing and time are required? What risks are involved? What strategies are required to deal with possible unplanned occurrences? The list goes on.

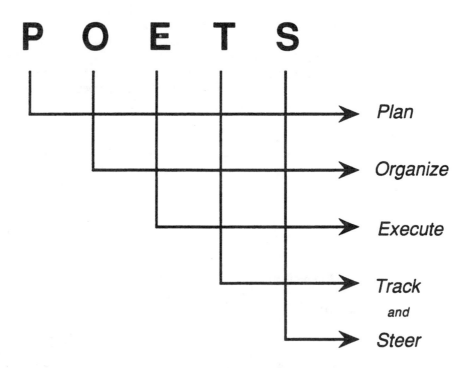

EFFECTIVE DIRECTION REQUIRES ESTABLISHING
WHAT IS GOING TO BE DONE
- AND THEN SEEING THAT IT ***IS*** DONE

Figure VII.2. Tracking and Steering a Project

Organize

The second basic step is an extension of the planning process. A careful analysis must be made of the various activities required in planning and executing a project in order to establish an appropriate project team structure and an inventory of skills that will be needed to complete the project. For every project activity required (e.g., programming, estimating, design, procurement, execution) There must eventually be a very clear definition of who is responsible and who has the authority to execute that activity. When the time comes, that person must have a very clear idea of the scope and quality that is expected and the time and cost available to complete the activity.

Execute

The methods by which the plan is executed or implemented are critical. No project manager (or other member of the project team) will be successful unless he or she understands the basic needs of human beings, their strengths and weaknesses, mental and social abilities, and how to weld a complex mixture of humans into a dynamic and productive team. Perhaps the single most important characteristic of a successful project manager is his or her ability to manage people.

Track

Continued tracking, reporting and position forecasting must take place during the project, especially during implementation. The results must be carefully checked against the original plan (or latest plan, if the plan has been formally updated), and any unacceptable deviations faithfully reported.

Steer

Unacceptable deviations from plan should immediately receive management's attention, either by re-allocation of resources or by modifications to the plan (with the Client's approval, of course, if his or her objectives are affected).

From this it can readily be seen that without a detailed plan there is no basis for comparison, no determination of deviation, and hence no satisfactory basis for corrective action or re-direction. Clearly then, what is needed is a system, and in this case a successful project management system is one which monitors and responds by a controlling action as early as possible after an event.

C. Input-Process-Output and the Feedback Loop

Whether or not project management is really an art or a science, modern project management does rely heavily on the science of systems to be effective. One of the most basic is the classic *Input-Process-Output* model with critical

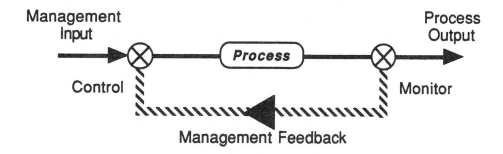

Figure VII.3. Traditional Management Feedback

feedback loop as illustrated in Figure VII.3. Some practical examples will help in the understanding of this control mechanism.

Consider a simple machine-to-machine system such as an electric furnace, or air conditioner. In these machines, the input is the electric power and the output is hot (or cold) air. These devices employ three essential control tools: namely,

1. A monitoring mechanism, in this case, a thermostat;
2. A comparative device, e.g., the thermostat signal with a set point or objective; and
3. A means for sending a corrective signal according to a preset formula.

The preset formula and corrective signal in its simplest form is on-off. When the temperature range is exceeded, the machine is automatically turned on upon receiving a corrective control signal, and remains on until the temperature is within range, when the next corrective signal dutifully turns the equipment off again.

Obviously, other more sophisticated formulae and signals are possible. In fact, this can be seen in the automobile example discussed in Section A above. In this case, based on the driver's judgment, directional control is supplied through the steering wheel and graduated control of the vehicle's speed is exercised by the gas and brake pedals.

D. The Project Control Cycle

Project management is a person-to-person system. In this case, the input is essentially requirements and design information, and resources of labor, materials and equipment. The output is the completed product(s) of the project. Along the way, the processing is done by workers with knowledge, skills and experience, who between them transform the raw data through plans to contracts (formal or informal) to execution and finally to termination, close-out or hand-over, as the case may be.

Control of this process is exercised through tracking, reporting and forecasting the output, comparing this to the project objectives and sending corrective signals to the input of data and resources. Thus, the project is steered towards an output that fully conforms to the project requirements. This management cycle is often referred to as the *project control cycle*, and is shown diagrammatically in Figure VII.4.

The project control cycle diagram shows five elements. Starting with developing or modifying the baseline plan, the cycle proceeds through the logical sequence of monitoring and reporting, analysis of the results, exercising control by modifying critical items, and re-forecasting as an input to the next control cycle update.

E. Characteristics of a Good PM Control System

In real life, the process of tracking and steering a project is continuous and rather more complex. The cycle described in Section D should continue through all of the project phases and never cease until the project is completed as shown in Figure VII.5.

In summary, a good project management control system should:

- facilitate detailed planning;
- be able to measure performance in relation to the plan and quickly report any deviations from the plan;
- be able to communicate planning and performance information to all parties involved; and
- identify objectives and highlight important operations leading to these objectives.

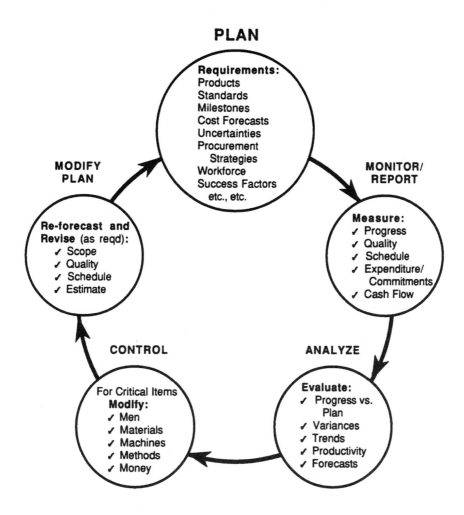

Figure VII.4. Project Control Cycle

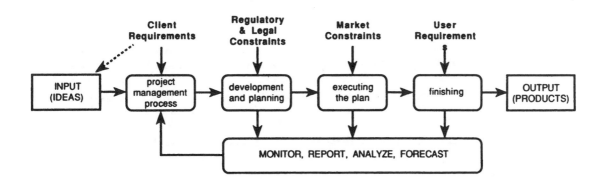

Figure VII.5. Project Control in Practice

F. The "S" Curve as a Management Control Tool

The "S" curve was briefly described in Chapter III.C as the progressive cumulative total of the level of effort required (or experienced) during the course of the project life cycle. As such, it provides a powerful technique for management control. For example, a typical curve is shown as curve "A" in Figure VII.6, and when plotted prior to commencement of the work, represents the planned

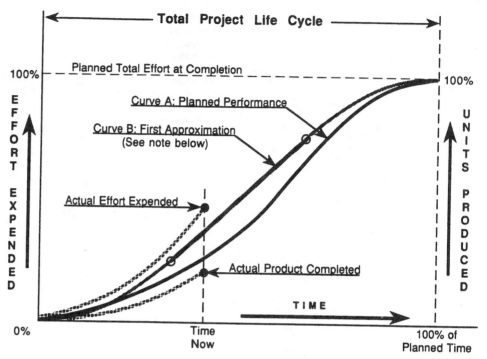

Figure VII.6. Project "S" Curves: A Powerful Management Control Tool

performance. If, as shown, corresponding scales of effort and units of production are both plotted vertically, it is possible to track concurrently the effort being input and the results being output. Figure VII.6 also shows a situation developing at Time-Now in which both productivity (actual effort expended) and the progress-to-date (actual units completed) are below expectation, and clearly call for project management action!

The effort expended is typically recorded in direct man-hours or direct costs consumed, but the product is often much more difficult to measure. This is in part because much of the product may still be in process at any given time, and require some subjective judgment. Consequently, where feasible, three or four *measurable* activities, preferably representing the bulk of the work on a project, are selected as major indicators of its health.

The precise shape of the planned performance curve, and particularly its resulting *steepest slope* representing the period of highest work intensity, will vary depending on the specific elements which comprise its component data. It can be plotted in either percentages or units as a function of time. At the macro project level it can be used to integrate all estimates of labor, equipment, material and overhead into one classic curve. A first approximation of this curve can be arrived at by plotting points represented by one-third of the time at one-quarter of the progress and two-thirds of the time at three-quarters of the progress, and joining these two points with a straight line. The "head and tail" of the "S" curve can then be roughed in with tangential spirals.[3] This is shown for comparison as curve "B" in the figure.

Changes in project scope or conditions change the shape of the curve, suggesting potential difficulty for the project team in meeting scheduled milestones and end dates. As indicated earlier, the results of continuous monitoring presented in this way can send strong signals of problems ahead needing urgent attention. While there are many more sophisticated curves for analyzing various aspects of the work, the "S" curve constitutes a fundamental management summary tool.[4]

G. Executive Control Points[5]

By combining the concepts of the Project Life Cycle with that of the Project Control cycle, it is possible to provide a higher level of control. In this approach, each phase of the project is treated as a mini-project in its own right, separated from its subsequent phase by an Executive Control Point. The Executive Control Point is so called because a high level of control is exercised only by the party having Executive Authority over the project (see Section V.A).

These points act like closed gates to the project team, and are only opened through Executive Approval. At these points, the project manager presents certain pre-determined "deliverables" to the Executive that will enable the Executive to make an informed decision on a "go" or "no-go" basis for further work. Approval to proceed would be granted only if the phase deliverables are satisfactory.

Thus, an opportunity is provided to the Executive for exercising a high level of control over the shape and timing of the project. The Executive can ensure that either the project is developing in a manner consistent with their objectives, or the project can be modified with a minimum upset, if the objectives have to be modified.

In this connection, it should be emphasized that the cost and delay associated with a change to the final project deliverables generally increases by many times in each succeeding phase. Perhaps as high as ten times for each succeeding phase.

These Executive Control Points also provide the opportunity for the Executive and project manager to provide a boost to the morale of the project team by infusing renewed excitement, enthusiasm and vigor. Equally, these formal approvals provide the project manager with the authority to drive the project to a successful conclusion of the ensuing phase. It is also an opportunity to ensure that the Executive is supportive of the project manager and is, in fact, proceeding in the right direction.

H. The Project Brief [6]

Undoubtedly, the most important Executive Control Point in the Project Life Cycle is reached at the conclusion of the development phase, because this marks the transition of the project from feasibility to implementation, from planning to realization, as shown in Figure II.2. At this point, a project "go" decision should be based on sound and well-documented information. This information should be presented in a comprehensive document sometimes referred to as the Project Bible, or Project Brief. It is the means whereby the Executive will know exactly what they are getting, or if not, at least where the areas of highest risks occur.

Thus, the Project Brief, once approved, becomes the prime source of reference for the project implementation phase. A good Project Brief should include:

· Executive summary
· General statement of business aims and objectives

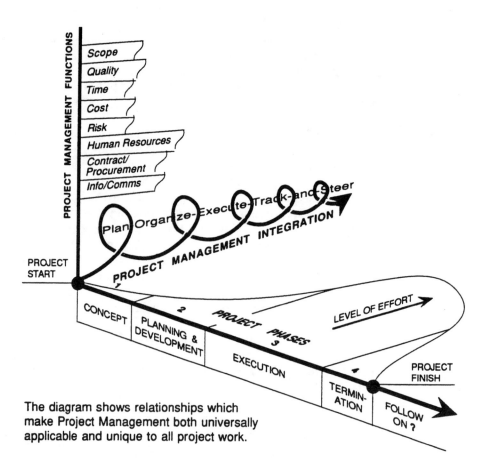

Figure VII.7. The Function-Process-Time Relationship in Project Management

- Justification
- Technical approach
- Statement of project scope and quality
- Legal or regulatory approvals, or requirements
- Preliminary design sketches or descriptions, flow diagrams, standards
- Project team organization
- Implementation schedule
- Procurement plan
- Project estimate and proposed budget
- Other resources required from the sponsoring organization (e.g., space, staff, equipment)
- Financial statement and economic projections
- Cash flow projections
- Alternatives
- Areas of uncertainty and risk

A good project brief will not be achieved without good project management practices in the upstream planning phases.

I. The Function-Process-Time Relationship[7]

This section is concluded with an attempt to show how the functions of project management, the project control process, and the project phases all relate to one another. These three fundamental components of project management may be viewed as a three-dimensional project system, as depicted in Figure VII.7.

In the diagram, the project life cycle is shown as usual on the X-axis, with its four phases and typical level-of-effort curve with which the phases are generally associated. On the Y-axis are the major project functions to be managed, which apply to any project, although they may vary in relative importance according to the field of project application or industry. The project's management must pay attention to each and every one of these, if they are to get the best out of the project. On the Z-axis is shown the higher frequency control cycle, which is also of an iterative nature. As time progresses, this cycle should become more and more focussed.

The point of the diagram is that, if the project's goals are to be successfully attained, this control cycle must be applied to each and every one of the major functions, as the project is progressively managed through its life cycle.

---

1. *PMBOK*, March 28, 1987, p4-3.
2. Ibid., p4-2.
3. R.M. Wideman, from unpublished text on construction progress monitoring.
4. S. Kutner, *Claims Management, Program Management: A Reference for Professionals*, Marcel Dekker, New York, 1989, p307.
5. R.M. Wideman, *Total Project Management of Complex Projects, Improving Performance with Modern Techniques*, Consultancy Development Centre, New Delhi, Indian, January 1990.
6. Ibid.
7. Ibid.

Chapter VIII   Towards Successful Project Management

A.   Project Success Equates to Participant Satisfaction

In PMI's definition of Project Management (see Chapter 2B), five objectives are identified. These consist of the four basic functional objectives of scope, quality, time and cost, and a fifth objective of a different dimension, namely, *participant satisfaction*. What is the rationale?

Interest in project management stems from a desire to manage projects better, to end up with a project which is more successful. But how can it be determined when a successful project has been achieved? Well, some things can be measured, but for the most part, it becomes a matter of opinion. Presumably, for a favorable opinion to be formed by those associated with a project, they must first be reasonably satisfied with it. Hence, *a successful project is one which has achieved participant satisfaction*.

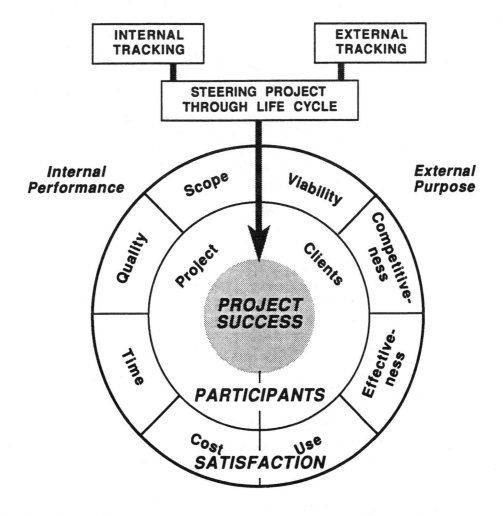

Figure VIII.1. The Success Target
Adapted from J. Pinto, PMJ, February 1988, p.69, by C. Quaife and M. Wideman, 2/23/91

Figure VIII.1 suggests a view which combines both internal and external environments, as discussed in Chapters V and VI. The trouble is, there are very many participants involved in most projects, and they view it, in all likelihood, from their individual perspectives. So, perhaps a successful project is one in which all the participants are *about equally satisfied* (proportional to their involvement). Of course, the cynic will say that the really successful project is one in which all the participants are about equally *dissatisfied*!

So clearly the old "triple constraint" view (that project success is comprised of three elements: budget, schedule, and performance — see Appendix A3) is not an accurate barometer of true success. The biggest problem is the common observation that perceived success varies depending upon who does the perceiving and at what point in time is this success being evaluated. For example, the project team's perceptions of success is always going to be subjected to a certain amount of bias (after all, their jobs may be on the line!).[1]

In the literature, there are many examples of projects which heavily overran budget and schedule, yet were subsequently considered great commercial successes, while others meeting the "triple constraint" proved to be downright failures. The differences are probably to be found in changes in the external environmental conditions, such as changes in the market or in stakeholder attitudes. In other words, the products of a project may be only a partial satisfaction of the sponsor's real needs (see Chapter III.E), because they are only part of a larger picture. This picture usually becomes better understood as the project proceeds. The moral is: *Doing the wrong thing right is never a success, but doing the right thing even half right may still be a winner!*

B. Who are the Project's Participants?

In Chapters V and VI, both the internal and external environments of the project and how these might be managed were discussed. In particular, in Chapter VI.D some effective strategies for dealing with the project's stakeholders were suggested. For purposes of this discussion, the project's participants and the project stakeholders are synonymous. For many projects, a primary and secondary listing of project participants might appear as follows:

1. Primary Participants

   - The project workforce
   - The project Users
   - The local community
   - The community at large
   - Special interest groups
   - Elected representatives and government administrators, and
   - The news media

2. Secondary Participants

   - Business and professional groups
   - Business media
   - Labor groups
   - Educators and school groups
   - Taxpayers
   - The industrial sector of the project

Come to think of it, that seems to cover just about everybody, so the strategies suggested in Chapter VI.D can make the listing more meaningful for a given project.

C. Can Project Success be Measured?

If the only objectives of the project are to get it completed within scope, cost and schedule, then certainly degrees of success can be measured against these parameters. But, as discussed above, if the real objective is to end up with a successful project, then important though these are, they are not the ultimate determinants of success. Heresy? Perhaps. But success, a difficult notion at best, is dependent upon satisfying the customers!

In fact, when measuring project success, one must consider the objectives of all stakeholders throughout the project life cycle and at all levels in the management hierarchy. Therefore, to believe that, with such a multitude of objectives, one can objectively measure the success of a project is somewhat of an illusion.[2]

Too often in the past, project managers have assumed that if, concentrating on the internal efficiency issues, they get the project out of the door on time and under budget, then they have achieved a success. This attitude is actually dangerous for project organizations that live or die by their ability to satisfy their customers.[3] At the very least, the importance of developing and updating the client's views in planning and assessing project success should not be overlooked. Perhaps equally important is the development of the client's requirements in a way that ensures that what the client asks for is what is really wanted.

In the long run, what really matters is whether the parties associated with, and affected by, a project are satisfied. Good schedule and cost performance alone means very little in the face of a poorly performing and poorly received end product.[4]

D. Three Basic Dimensions of Project Success

In attempting to deal with the problems associated with understanding and measuring project success, Dr. Jeffrey Pinto, an ardent PMI supporter, has done research with separate data bases which look at both sides of the coin: project success, and project failure. He concludes that clients (in this context, both sponsors and users) must be made a much bigger part of the equation for determining success, than has been the case to date. As a result of a 1989 working paper,[5] Pinto concluded that *project success* comprises three basic dimensions: namely, the *implementation process*; the *perceived value* of the project; and the clients' *acceptance and use* of the project.

The first dimension, the Implementation Process, concerns the *internal efficiency* with which the project was developed and includes measures of traditional budget and schedule issues. This dimension is most readily assessed by the project team.

The second dimension, the project's Perceived Value, needs to be jointly planned and defined by the project team and the client. Both have a stake in creating a useful project. However, beauty is often in the eye of the beholder and what may be viewed as valuable by the project team may be useless to the client!

Project Success Measure	Comprised of	As perceived by
Implementation Process	Internal efficiency: conformance to scope, quality, schedule & cost requirements	Project team
Perceived Value	Positive impact and potential for clients to improve performance	Project team and clients
Acceptance and Use	Acceptability to clients and actual usefulness	Clients

The third dimension is that of Clients' Acceptance and Use of the project. This dimension can only be assessed by the clients. However, this measure of success is very difficult to pin down because it is affected by the element of time. A project that is valuable today, may not necessarily be so tomorrow.

These three measures are tabulated below.[6]

E. Determinants of Project Success and Failure

Factors Critical to Success

In research by Slevin and Pinto, a number of factors were found to be critical to project success.[7]

Factors generally within the control of the project team:

a. *Project Mission:* Initial clarity of goals and general directions
b. *Top Management Support:* Willingness of top management to provide the necessary resources and authority/power for project success
c. *Project/Schedule Plans:* A detailed description of the individual action steps required for implementation
d. *Client Consultation:* Communication, consultation and active listening to all impacted parties
e. *Personnel:* Recruitment, selection, and training of the necessary personnel for the project team
f. *Technical Tasks:* Availability of the required technology and expertise to accomplish the specific technical action steps
g. *Client Acceptance:* The act of "selling" the final project to its ultimate intended users
h. *Monitoring and Feedback:* Timely provision of comprehensive control information at each stage in the implementation process
i. *Communication:* The provision of an appropriate network and necessary data to all key actors in the project implementation
j. *Trouble-shooting:* Ability to handle unexpected crises and deviations from plan

Other critical factors often considered beyond the control of the project team:

k. *Characteristics of the Project Team Leader:* Competence of the project leader (administratively, interpersonally, and technically) and the amount of authority available to perform his or her duties
l. *Power and Politics:* The degree of political activity within the organization and perception of the project as furthering an organization member's self-interests
m. *Environmental Events:* The likelihood of external organizational and environmental factors impacting on the operations of the project team, either positively or negatively
n. *Urgency:* The perception of the importance of the project or the need to implement the project as soon as possible

How to Ensure Failure

For the masochist, here are some good ways to ensure project failure:

a. Make sure that the project team is assembled before appointment of the project manager
b. Make sure that your project has a lofty objective, uncluttered by specifics
c. Avoid changes to the project by keeping clear of the project's stakeholders
d. Run the project democratically throughout, and avoid visible authority
e. Give everyone an opportunity to learn on the job, and keep clear of expert advice
f. Allow each team player to make their own technical, quality, schedule and cost decisions independent of any project objectives

g. Keep everyone on their toes by identifying a daily crisis
h. Abdicate all dealings with outside parties to someone at a lower level
i. Rotate this responsibility, so that everyone gains experience
j. Make sure that expenditures are controlled by the company accountant
k. Keep cost and schedule information strictly confidential, and don't let it interfere with project progress
l. Don't upset top management by insisting on support for the project

F. A Self-Test for Project Success

The following questions[8] suggest a useful self-test for the project manager who takes pride in a successful project. Each question may be rated on a scale of 1 to 7, with the best projects taking the highest total marks! The overall intent is to determine the extent to which the project objectives are identified, reviewed and met.

Internal Factors:

This project:
a. Will meet/has met its defined scope
b. Will conform/has conformed to its quality requirements
c. Will/has come in on schedule
d. Will/has come in on budget
e. As being developed, looks as if it will work/did work as developed
f. Given the problem for which it is intended, appears to be the best choice amongst the alternatives available
g. Will provide/has provided results representing definite improvement over clients' previous conditions

External Factors:

a. The intended clients will/do make use of this project
b. Other important clients, i.e., those directly affected by the project, will/do make use of it
c. We are confident that non-technical start-up problems will be/were minimal, because the project will be/was accepted by its intended clients
d. We are/were satisfied with the process by which the product/facility is/was being brought into existence
e. This project benefitted/will benefit the intended clients directly, through increased user efficiency or effectiveness
f. Use of this project will lead/has led to improved, or more effective, decision making or performance by its intended clients
g. This project will/did have a positive impact on all of its stakeholders

G. Vision, Creativity, Discovery and Judgment[9]

Vision. The project manager and his or her team must have a clear mental picture of the outcome of their project at all times, a developing understanding of all the steps involved in getting there, and their logical sequence. It is well, too, to have a good picture of the characteristics of the environment in which the project is being launched, and the impact that the project will have on that environment.

Creativity. During the life of a project, the project team will face many ideas, suggestions and hurdles, with even more solutions which appear and disappear in chaotic piles of data, and a jumble of contradictory statistics and reports of expert opinions. Each offers its own merits, assumptions, limitations and risks. Managers need to cut through the chaos to reach a solution appropriate for the project, often with insufficient information. The key lies in his/or her ability to think creatively in each situation and to act boldly.

Discovery. In the course of a project, but especially in the concept and development phases, there is often a real need to explore new ideas relevant to the project. In these phases, ideas should be openly suggested, tested and improved with little risk. The resulting discovery should be assessed against what is important in terms of project success.

Judgment. Appraisal and deduction are intrinsic elements of an individual's decision making process which are inevitably influenced by circumstantial factors such as (a) self-image, including irrelevant emotions and sometimes distorted impressions of one's own capabilities; (b) judgment by others taken for granted, but which itself requires distinction between emotional blame or criticism and clear, rational assessment; and (c) collective judgments which act to restrict the leader's freedom of action. Together, these factors may act to realign constructive energies away from real project needs. They may also act to kill curiosity and the courage to try new ideas, or take calculated risks in the project environment.

Project success depends to a considerable degree on a keen awareness, a rational analysis of current organizational circumstances, designing and taking the necessary steps to create and maintain a viable all-encompassing project plan, and faithfully executing its content.

1. J. Pinto, summary provided in letter dated June 5, 1989.
2. A. de Wit, Measurement of Project Success, *International Journal of Project Management*, Vol. 6, No. 3, August 1988, p164.
3. J. Pinto, summary provided in letter dated June 5, 1989.
4. B.N. Baker, D.C. Murphy and D. Fisher, Factors Affecting Project Success, in D.I. Cleland and W.R. King (eds.) *Project Management Handbook*, New York: Van Nostrand Reinhold, 1983, p669-685.
5. J.K. Pinto and J.E. Prescott, Planning and Tactical Factors in the Project Implementation Process, Working Paper 89-07, University of Maine, December 1988.
6. J. Pinto, summary provided in a letter dated June 5, 1989.
7. D.P. Slevin and J.K. Pinto, The Project Implementation Profile: New Tool for Project Managers, *Project Management Journal*, September 1986, p57.
8. After J.K. Pinto and D.P. Slevin, Project Success: Definitions and Measurement Techniques, *Project Management Journal*, Vol. XIX, February 1988, p72.
9. S. Zuberi, thoughts contributed in a letter dated June 5, 1990.

Part D   Conclusions

Chapter IX   Summary And Conclusions

A.   A Strategy for the Future[1]

As of this writing, a number of concerns have been identified relating to the PMBOK, and which are currently receiving attention. These include:

1. The development of a satisfactory model which ties together the major components of the PMBOK and, indeed, the different models currently in vogue
2. Higher visibility of the Project Life Cycle as a fundamental part of project management and of PMBOK
3. Greater consistency in the project management functions, and particularly intheir terminologies
4. Consistency in the breakdowns of the PM functions and their component processes
5. Development of a breakdown for each of the Integrative PM Functions
6. Increased focus on the integrative nature of project management, and
7. Greater attention to the influence of environmental factors on projects
8. Better correlation between the Function Charts and the PMP certification Official Study Guides
9. Development of criteria covering eligibility for inclusion of Integrative PM Functions

The foregoing comprise the first steps of a longer-term strategy to improve the current PMBOK. Issues to be addressed in this longer-term strategy include:

1. How generalized could or should the PMBOK be? There is the possibility that a PMBOK which is general enough to be applicable to all projects might be too general to be really useful to either educators or practitioners.
2. If the generic PMBOK forms the core for educational programs, the normal situation in both education and practice will be that the exemplar and actual projects will be tied to specific industries and/or technologies. Therefore, industry/technology-specific check-listing materials will be necessary to cover relevant projects in both education and practice.
3. The assembly of industry/technology-specific Body of Knowledge materials is both a worthy and necessary undertaking in its own right in helping to build professionalism in project management
4. A major review and upgrade of the generic PMBOK

PMI is in a unique position to initiate the task of collecting, collating, editing and augmenting existing materials, and in making them available to all interested educators and practitioners. Additionally, PMI is best placed to initiate the generation and distribution of new materials in relevant areas not already covered.

B.   PMI's Professional Leadership Opportunity

The public, private and academic sectors are becoming increasingly involved in managing change through the medium of projects. These projects are becoming more complex and increasingly require expert management from a limited pool of trained people. The Project Management Institute sees improvement in the management of projects as the essential prerequisite to improved product quality and performance, and hence better response to public and private needs.

PMI has in place a current (1990) five year plan in which the principal goal is to move the practice of project management into the arena of professional recognition as soon as possible. The salient features of this plan include:

- Expanded opportunity for project management practitioners to become Project Management Professionals (PMP) through the PMI certification (testing) process, pioneered by PMI since 1982 and being continuously upgraded;
- Preparation of broad-based educational material that will provide the means for learning the fundamentals of good project management practice as embodied in the Project Management Body of Knowledge (PMBOK) and associated standards to improve professional knowledge, skills and attitudes;
- Development of programs to promote standardization and quality in the proliferation of privately- and publicly-sponsored training courses in the field of project management;
- Expanded services in accreditation and re-accreditation of graduate level university degree programs in project management;
- Stimulation of research to enhance and advance the state-of-the-art in project management concepts, processes, and techniques.[2]

The future project manager will be a business person: one who will have the ability to appreciate and use technology advantageously; one who will understand the needs of people in whatever social setting exists. Worldwide projects will be directed towards infrastructure, industrialization, consumer goods, and basic needs. Domestic projects will stress infrastructure, high-technology, environment, defense, and space programs. The project-driven organization will recognize the authority of the project manager, and from the ranks, select the executives of tomorrow.[3]

C. PMI on a Global Stage

Project managers are the key not only to engineering firms but also to the whole world of work in the 1990s and beyond. Many business and thought leaders are predicting that more and more, businesses will be organized around projects and will bring people on board only for the duration of a particular contract ... The person who can assemble and motivate high-performance project teams will be the impact player of the next business decade ... Project managers need both training and development because they are a unique breed, requiring equal doses of management and leadership skills.[4]

PMI's programs are focussed on the practice of effective project management, in all areas of application, in any culture, anywhere.

---

1. A. Stretton, abstracted from A Consolidation of the PMBOK Framework and Functional Components, *Project Management Journal*, December 1989, p13.
2. H. Padgham, abstracted from Concerns of the Institute, *PM NETwork*, Vol. IV, No. 4, May 1990.
3. J.H. Loweree, *Project Management: A Reference for Professionals*, Marcel Dekker, Inc., 1989, p1086.
4. G. Davis, a principal of Davis & Dean, as quoted in the PMI Puget Sound Chapter Newsletter, March 1990.

Appendices

Appendix A

A Historical Perspective

1. Introduction

PMI was launched in 1969, as a non-profit organization dedicated to advancing the state-of-the-art in the management of projects. More recently, this dedication has been articulated in a statement of PMI's mission, which is:

To be the leading recognized professional and technical association in advancing the state of the art of program and project management, and
To be achieved through the development and dissemination of the theory and practice of effective management of resources in reaching project goals.

This mission provides a central focus for PMI's supporting objectives and consequent activities. The identification, development and dissemination of this knowledge is therefore only a part of the overall activity of the Institute, albeit an important cornerstone of many of those activities. This relationship is shown conceptually in Figure A1.

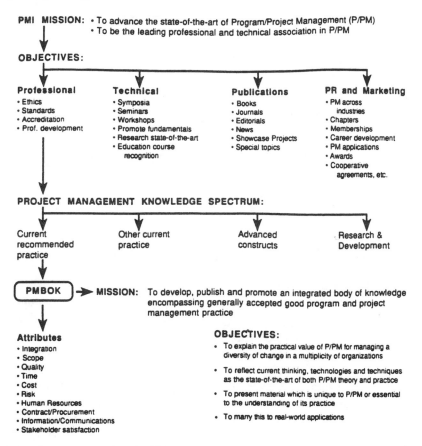

Figure A1. PMI's Activity Structure and PMBOK

The figure shows that project management knowledge may be represented by a spectrum ranging from current practice through to advanced research and development. However, the focus of the generic PMBOK is on an integrated body of knowledge which encompasses generally accepted (i.e., current) good program and project management practice.

Nevertheless, if current practice is to advance, the remainder of the spectrum must receive attention, and, over time, feed into the generic PMBOK. Moreover, there will be areas of project management application wherein other practices are appropriate, but which are not necessarily considered to be generic at this time. This concept is shown diagrammatically in Figure A2, and the relative scopes of the generic PMBOK, industry-specific applications, and the institutes of higher learning PMBOKs should be noted.

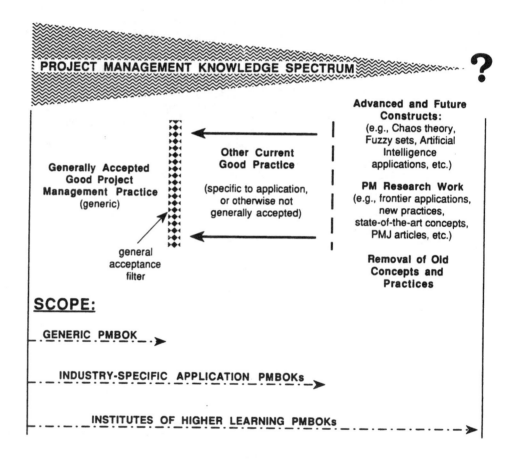

Figure A.2. The Scope of Project Management Knowledge

2. Early Work on a Body of Knowledge[1]

The concept of standards was first introduced at the Montreal Symposium of 1976. However, it was not until 1981 that the PMI Board accepted a proposal for a project to develop a code of Ethics, Standards for the body of knowledge of project management, and an Accreditation program for the recognition of institutions of higher learning. It became known as the original ESA project, and its objective was to establish project management as a unique discipline and independent profession. The report was published in the Project Management Quarterly in August 1983, and the first members were tested for Certification in October 1984.

Interest in Certification brought the knowledge standards under much closer scrutiny and, inevitably, shortcomings were identified. At the same time, some significant publications became available in the form of PMI symposia papers, articles, and handbooks, as well as some public text books authored by PMI members. Therefore, in 1984, the PMI Board established a project designed "To capture the knowledge applied to project management by PMI members, to do so within the existing ESA framework and to present it in simple but comprehensive terms."

The results of the voluntary work of a large number of PMI members were scrutinized and validated at a special workshop held at the Denver Symposium of 1985. Following some further work, the results were accepted-in-principle by the PMI Board in April 1986, and published for comment in a Special Summer Issue of the Project Management Journal in August 1986. The revised text, which became known as the PMBOK, was approved by the PMI Board in March 1987, and published in the *PM NETwork* in August 1987.

3. Some Early Models

A variety of models were considered by the Denver group. One of the earliest models is shown in Figure A3, relating schedule, cost and technical performance. However, while useful, it is very limited in that technical performance itself consists of two independent variables, namely, scope and quality, and the model should be square rather than triangular! Moreover, the integrative functions of project management are quite independent of, and cut across, these basic functions. The value of a two or more dimensional matrix then

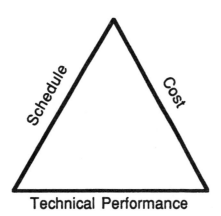

Figure A3. Project Elements

became obvious; one dimension consisting of the basic project functions, and the other dimension consisting of the integrative functions.

The desirability of adding a third dimension for the project life cycle, as shown in Figure A.4, then became apparent. A case could be made for adding further dimensions. The system environmental level, the system technical environment, or even the breakdown into processes, activities, tools and techniques (described in Appendix B) could all be added so that the PMBOK might well be represented by a multidimensional matrix. However, from a practical point of view, the advantages of these added dimensions may be minor, and their existence can be recognized within the descriptions of the body of knowledge.

4. Matrices and Similar Models[2]

The Project Management Matrix Model

If the objective is to relate the basic project management functions to the integrative functions by means of a matrix chart, then the Denver group soon found considerable disagreement as to what elements are needed to complete the picture, and on which of the two dimensions they should appear. There seemed to be an almost unlimited number of management functions which might be included. The final consensus of the meeting produced the model shown in Figure A5.

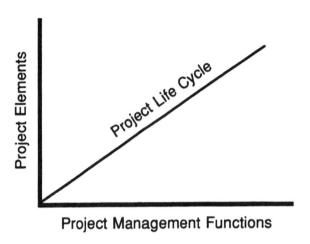

Figure A.4. Project Management Three-Dimensional Matrix

The Know-How Continuum Model[3]

An attempt to depict the environment of project management is shown in Figure A.6. This figure shows the role of the PMBOK as a vehicle for the creation of change between General Management and Technical Management. It is thus complementary to the Venn diagram shown in Figure IV.1, Chapter IV.C. The diagram may be explained as follows:

As marked at the top, the light gray background is intended to portray the whole know-how continuum necessary to conduct industry and business successfully. This includes all sectors, public and private. The continuum ranges from the know-how of general management on the left, through project management, to technical management on the right.

The series of strips immediately below are intended to elaborate on the content of each. The central overlay circle encompasses the process and control of project management, involving the four basic objectives or constraints of scope, quality, time and cost, which are at the four tips of the star. As every project manager knows, these objectives or constraints are inextricably interwoven in ways that tend to change during the course of the project life cycle.

The diagram notes that for the project team to function effectively, "PM staff must have sufficient understanding of the various specialist disciplines to appreciate project requirements and issues. They must be able to communicate appropriate direction and means of conflict resolution to these specialists in order to reach a successful project conclusion." One might add that because of technical bias, specialists frequently have difficulty in becoming good project managers, unless they have had good project management training.

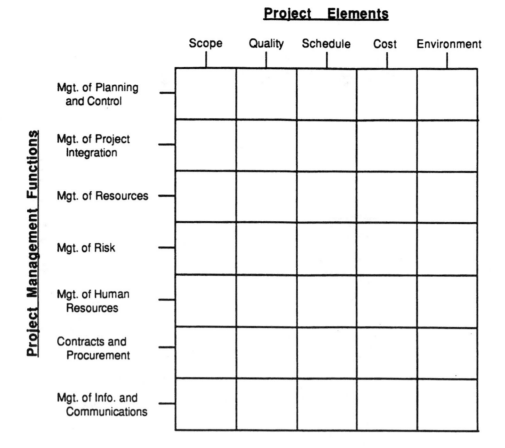

Figure A.5. Project Management Matrix Model

This "sufficient understanding" is represented by the "fingers" which reach into the areas of general management on the left, and into the technical management on the right. The extent to which they should do so is reflected by the strip at the bottom of the diagram. The darker gray area on the left is therefore the knowledge which every project manager should have, while the darker gray area on the right represents the extent of the specific technical knowledge required. It is this latter which makes the project manager a specialist in a given area of application.

A Simple Work Breakdown Model

Subsequent to the Denver group's workshop, but prior to PMI's formal publication of the PMBOK, the reports were reviewed for purposes of summary and recommendations by a PM Framework Group.[4]

The resulting article suggested that the need for a Framework model is evidenced by the need to answer the question "What is Project Management?" It suggested that inability to give a consistent answer to this question demonstrates the need. It concluded that the Framework model should:

- Describe how Project Management is different from other types of management.
- Establish criteria for determining what constitutes a Functional Component.
- Identify the present components of Project Management and their dynamic interaction.

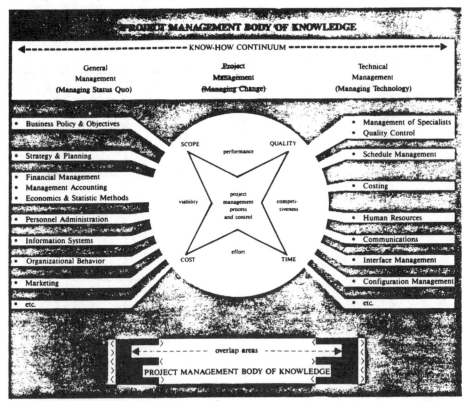

NOTE: The overlap areas infer that the project management staff must have sufficient understanding of the various specialist disciplines to appreciate project requirements and issues. They must also be able to communicate appropriate direction and means of conflict resolution to these specialists in order to reach a successful project conclusion.

Figure A.6. Project Management Body of Knowledge

- Describe the appropriate applications of Project Management and its benefits.
- Provide an authoritative lexicon of the technical terms of Project Management.

Based on the information and views then current, a Project Management Framework Chart was produced as shown in Figure A.7.

5. Concerns and Current Thinking

Weaknesses Exposed

At a PMBOK (Standards) Committee Workshop held at the Atlanta Symposium in 1989, many weaknesses which merit attention were identified in the current PMBOK materials, namely:

1. The lack of a satisfactory framework or model which ties together the major components of the PMBOK, and indeed which ties together the different models currently proposed;
2. Inadequate coverage of the project life cycle as a fundamental part of project management and the PMBOK;
3. Inconsistencies in establishing just what are the Project Management (PM) Functions, and in the terminology used to describe them;

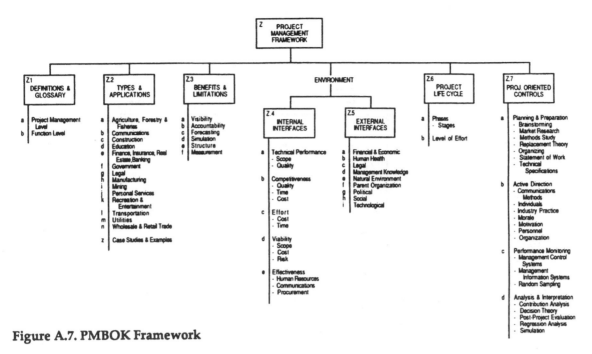

Figure A.7. PMBOK Framework

4. Inconsistencies in the breakdowns of PM functions into their component processes;
5. Inadequate focus on the integrative nature of project management;
6. Inadequate attention to the influence on projects of environmental factors.

For example, the current PMBOK has detailed Function charts for eight PM Functions, which break each down into component processes, activities and relevant techniques. These are presently done in quite an uneven way, and would benefit from some basic coordination. Three additional functions or "elements" appear in several of the existing matrix models, but are not discussed in detail in the text. One additional element appears in one model only. In addition, there is considerable confusion in terminologies, with two and sometimes three descriptions. Finally, there are evidently some differences of opinion as to which of the above properly qualify as PM Functions.

A 3-D Integrative PMBOK Framework Model

It has been suggested that the governing feature of any project — and sometimes the least understood — is the project life cycle itself. Because of the "fractal" phenomena of project management discussed in Chapter 3A, it is not unreasonable to array the contents of the project management functions along the life cycle dimension. This possibility was discussed in a paper in the December 1989, *Project Management Journal*,[5] from which Figure A.8 is reproduced. As the paper notes, while this is a somewhat inexact process, it does suggest ways for getting more uniform and useful breakdowns of the PM functions into their primary processes. When displayed in this way, many of the PMBOK functions show a natural progression, and also highlight some possibly missing processes.

However, Human Resources and Information/Communications do not seem to respond to this approach, which raises the interesting question of whether indeed they should, or whether they are essentially different. Even so, it is possible to suggest progressive sets of activities for these functions, as shown.

The paper, which should be required reading for all students of PMBOK, goes on to propose a three-dimensional integrative PMBOK Framework model, as shown in Figure A.9. As can be seen, the end of the model provides an opportunity to display some of the more important internal interfaces. This is demonstrated by the suggested interface connections shown in Figure A.10.

Function Chart Processes / Project Management Functions	PROJECT LIFE CYCLE						
	Phase 1 **Concept**	**Phase 2** **Development**		**Phase 3** **Execution**		**Phase 4** **Finishing**	
SCOPE	Conceptual Development	Scope Statement	Work Authorization	Scope Reporting	Control Systems	Project Close-out	
QUALITY	OVERALL Quality Philosophy	Q/A (MANAGERIAL) Technical Specifications	Technical Administration	Progress Review	Q/C (TECHNICAL) Technical Support	Evaluation Methods	
TIME	Time Planning	Time Estimating		Time Scheduling	Time Control	Time Applications	
COST	Cost Estimating & Forecasting	Cost Budgeting		Cost Controls		Cost Applications	
RISK	IDENTIFICATION Risk Classification	Insurable; Impact Analysis	MITIGATION Response Planning	Response System		Data Applications	
HUMAN RESOURCES	(Forming)	(Storming)	(Norming)	(Performing)		(Adjourning)*	
CONTRACT / PROCUREMENT	Objective	Information Systems	Procurement Identification	Acquisition Process	Contract Administration	Post Contract Evaluation	
INFORMATION / COMMUNICATIONS	(Data Input)	(Speculation)	(Analysis)	(Discussion)		(Solution)**	

* Suggested by A. Stretton, after Tuckman, 1985   ** Suggested by M. Wideman, 1990

Figure A.8. Project Management Function Processes Arrayed Along the Project Life Cycle
After A. Stretton, August 1989, Rev. 1/10/91

The purpose of the model is to provide a basis for needed rationalization of the PMBOK. For example, Project Integration is placed in a central position at the junction of the core and facilitating PM function streams, and indicates that it applies throughout the project life cycle. The model also specifically incorporates project management environmental factors in the form of Internal and External Interfaces, which are discussed in Chapters V and VI.

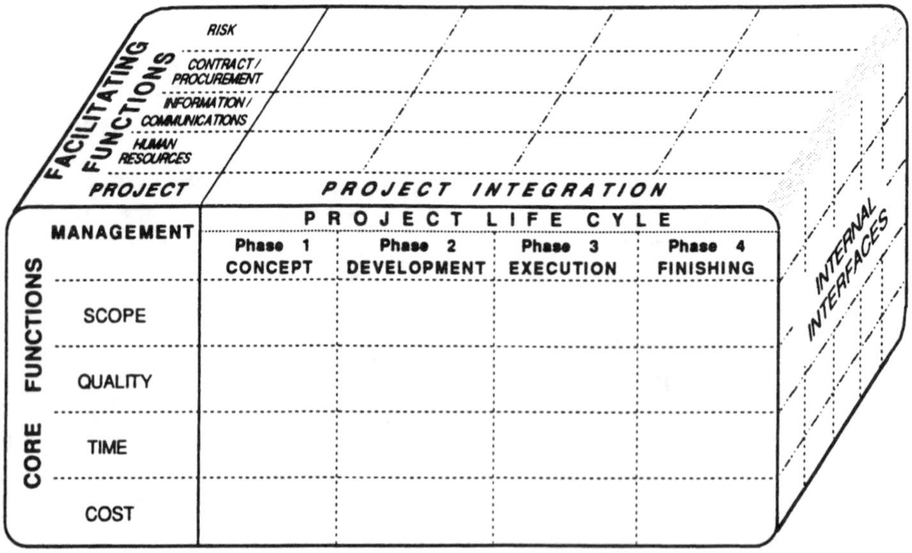

Figure A.9. A Three-Dimensional Integrative Model of the Project Management Process
After A. Stretton, August 1989, Rev. 1/10/91

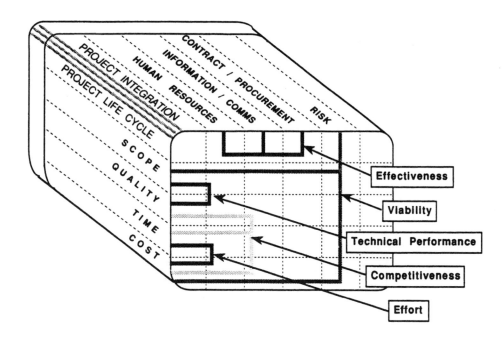

Figure A.10. Project Environment: Important Internal Interfaces

The model does not introduce new material but could provide a superior frame of reference for making better use of the existing materials for both education and practice. For example, in education it suggests possibilities for teaching project management in a holistic mode rather than as isolated subjects, which students are somehow expected to integrate for themselves. In particular, the centrality of the project life cycle helps provide a sense of realism and order, because it focuses attention on where and how various functions come into play in progressing a project through the sequential phases of its life cycle.

1. *PMBOK*, March 28, 1987, p0-1.
2. Ibid., p2-5.
3. Ibid., p1-5.
4. Philip C. Nunn, PMP, *PMBOK*, March 28, 1987, Section 3-1.
5. Alan Stretton, A Consolidation of the PMBOK Framework and Functional Components, *Project Management Journal*, December 1989, p5.

Appendix B

Establishing PMBOK Terms Of Reference

The form and content of the Project Management Body of Knowledge is a subject which has received increasing attention in recent years, as it is properly felt that there should be rigorous support as to whether particular material should be included or excluded. This is discussed at length in Chapter IV.C, D, and E. However, the basis of PMBOK goes back to the definition of project and the definition of project management itself (see Chapter II.A and B).

Project management is complex, and its body of knowledge is to be dealt with satisfactorily, then a framework is needed within which it is possible to organize and reference the various subtopics. By consensus, the 1985 Overview Committee developed the following terms of reference:[1]

Objective:

- To establish a systematic model/framework/structure for the PMBOK

Purpose:

- To organize and classify
- To integrate
- To correlate
- To store and retrieve
- To build on what we have

Characteristics:

- Simple
- Logical
- Saleable
- Comprehensive
- Compatible
- Systematic
- Understandable

The Overview Committee quickly recognized that a two-dimensional breakdown structure is too restrictive for purposes of adequately describing the necessary interdependencies and interrelationships between the various project management functions. It also recognized the need to examine the scope and boundaries of the PMBOK. This led to a number of conceptual models, which are discussed in Chapter IV.

Ideally, each function content should reflect increasing detail progressing downwards through the chart. Thus, the content of each function would appear as follows:[2]

M. H. Price has suggested a set of criteria for the inclusion (or exclusion) of a function based on the assumption that there is a common set of characteristics.[3] Each characteristic defines a start-up task and results in information which can be consolidated to meet most of the requirements of the project management plan (or plans). The characteristics which have thereby evolved are:

Level	Description	Content
0	Profession	the complete project management matrix
1	Function	Scope, Quality, Time, etc.
2	Process	the specific series of activities which lead to an output which is the title of the process item in the box o n the chart, e.g., budgeting, scheduling, organization, quality in design, etc. In other words, the "what" in "what is project management?"
3	Activity	the series of tasks which lead to the specific process output. In other words, the "how to get there"
4	Techniques	the specific tools available to aid or accomplish the activity

1. Every function is composed of one or more activities for which a specific organization structure can be identified or developed.

2. There is a specific set of deliverable products or services which can be identified with the function.

3. There is a specific set of work packages and tasks which can be assigned to each activity in the function.

4. A specific set of specifications or standards can be identified or developed for the products or services provided within the function.

5. A specific set of personnel can be identified to perform the work of the function.

6. Responsibility for each work package or task in the function can be specifically assigned to an activity or person.

7. Specific procedures can be identified or developed for management of the function or its component activities.

8. Equipment, software, data or other resources needed to perform the function can be identified.

9. Training needed to perform the function can be identified.

10. Job descriptions can be developed for each person performing the work of the function.

11. Specific criteria can be identified or developed against which to evaluate the performance of the work of the function.

12. A set of management information system inputs and outputs can be identified for use in monitoring progress within the function.

---

1. *PMBOK*, March 28, 1987, p0-3.
2. Ibid., p4-2.
3. Abstracted from correspondence by M.H. Price, PMI member, ©. July 1990.

Appendix C

Project Management Applications

1. Appropriate Use of Project Management

Whether project management is appropriate to the conduct of a particular effort may be analyzed by examining its characteristics: namely,[1]

- meets project definition by having defined objectives to be achieved, which will signal completion
- unique, or relatively rare
- time and cost are critical
- resources are limited
- resources must be shared between organizational units
- large
- technically complex
- technology is new
- specific ad hoc opportunities or problems must be dealt with
- results are critical or especially important
- has strong top management support
- coordination across functional boundaries required
- outside goods and services must be coordinated
- single point responsibility and reporting required
- single point representation to the customer required
- quick response to changing conditions required
- organizational disruption must be minimized
- multiple regulatory approvals require coordination
- other concurrent projects exist

2. Range and Diversity of Projects

Examples of project management applications abound. Their range and diversity may be illustrated by the following:[2]

- Design, engineering, and construction of a highway, bridge, dam, canal, building, etc.
- Design and implementation of an urban (or rural) development program
- Design of a military project, e.g., submarine, fighter aircraft, tank, or military communications system
- Building a nuclear power plant
- Research and development of a new machine tool
- Development of a new product or manufacturing process
- Reorganizing a corporation
- Implementing a new administrative system
- Launching a marketing initiative
- Landing a man on the moon and returning safely to earth

The foregoing are perhaps the most obvious. Examples of application which occur more frequently include:

- Producing a stage play
- Writing a book
- Restoring an antique car
- Designing a new teaching course
- Building (or remodelling) a house
- Getting married (or divorced)

3. Typical Industries Using Project Management

- Aerospace
- Agriculture/Foods
- Amusements
- Automotive
- Banking
- Chemicals/Petroleum/Pharmaceuticals/Rubber and Plastics/Leather/Metals
- Communications/Media
- Electronics/Instruments/Computers/Software
- Engineering/Design/Construction
- Finance/Insurance/Real Estate
- Government and Civil Service
- Hotels
- Lumber and Wood Products/Pulp and Paper
- Mining
- Museums/Zoos
- Printing/Publishing
- Resource Industries
- Services:Educational/Health/Legal/Social
- Ships/Boats/Marine
- Software/Hardware Development
- Stone/Clay/Glass/Concrete
- Telecommunications
- Textiles
- Transportation/Railroads
- Utilities/Energy
- Volunteer Organizations
- Wholesale/Retail Trade

4. Potential Domains for Project Management[3]

Grouped by Broad *Functional* Similarity and Suggested PMBOK Affinity

These domains cut across both manufacturing and services industries, are present in most organizations whether separate or combined, and can benefit from project management principles and practices:

• Architecture/Engineering/Design	Scope
• Construction	"
• Maintenance	"
• Manufacturing Operations	"
• Research and Development	"
• Environmental/Safety Protection	Quality
• Quality Assurance/Control/Inspection	"
• Corporate Planning	Time
• Finance/Accounting	Cost
• Fund Raising	"
• Insurance/Risk	Risk
• Personnel/HR Development/Training	H/R
• Purchasing/Procurement/Legal	C/P

• Communications/Public Relations	Info/Comms
• Information Systems/Records Management	"
• Marketing/Sales	"

Grouped by Broad *Product* Similarity

Projects in these groupings of industry domains may be expected to have similar working environments:

- Aerospace
- Agriculture/Foods
- Air/Land/Sea Transportation
- Amusements/Museums/Zoos
- Chemicals/Pharmaceuticals/Petroleum/Plastics and Rubber
- Commercial/Institutional/Residential Construction
- Communications/Media
- Computers/Electronics/Instruments/Software
- Government/Defense
- Lumber/Wood/Pulp and Paper Products
- Manufacturing: Automotive/Concrete/Clay/Glass/Leather/Metals/Stone/Textiles
- Marine/Boats/Ships
- Political Campaigning
- Printing/Publishing
- Private Services: Financial/Insurance/Legal/Real Estate
- Public Services: Educational/Health/Social/Tourism
- Travel Accommodation
- Utilities
- Volunteer Organizations
- Wholesale/Retail Trade

5. Potential Advantages

- Appropriate where effort qualifies as a project
- Improved scope definition
- Resource optimization
- Results orientation
- Greater quality conformance
- Higher reliability
- Reduced time
- Reduced cost
- Improved risk handling
- Greater team spirit
- Increased individual morale
- Improved functional integration
- Increased visibility
- Better control
- Higher chance of success
- Better customer relations

6. Traps to Avoid

- Inappropriate where effort does not qualify as a project
- Disorganization
- Disruptive conflict
- Special leadership skills missing
- Project management knowledge missing
- Trade-offs not understood
- Timely decisions missing

- Goodwill missing
- An appropriate cultural environment not established
- More difficult than traditional management
- Success not absolutely assured

7. When Not to Use[4]

- The business products or services are highly standardized
- The production processes are routine or seldom change
- The standard organizational framework is effective in making strategic and key operating decisions
- The technology is stable and well within the state-of-the-art
- The political, social, economic, technological and competitive environments are stable
- Projects are not an integral part of the organization's operations and do not require project management techniques
- The entity is small and the same results can be accomplished through the functional organization, even though "informal" project management techniques may be used

---

1. After L. Stuckenbruck, The Implementation of Project Management, PMI, 1981, p17-18.
2. After D.I. Cleland, *Project Management – Strategic Design and Implementation*, Tab Books, Inc., PA, 1990, p9.
3. Letter J.R. Thatcher to A. Stretton, February 8, 1990.
4. After D.I. Cleland, *Project Management – Strategic Design and Implementation*, Tab Books, Inc., PA, 1990, p51.

Appendix D

Project Management Learning

Figure D.1[1] shows one model of project management learning covering the range from art to science, its corresponding range of content, and how these progressive levels might be conveyed to members of the profession for the betterment of project performance. At the same time, PMI has identified a range of instruction methods which have been placed into four distinct categories: (1) lecture, (2) case study, (3) simulation, and (4) on-the-job training. These four progressive types of learning roughly approximate to the first four levels shown in the figure. It is suggested that the material studied should, at the same time, progress from "generic" project management to "industry-specific."[2]

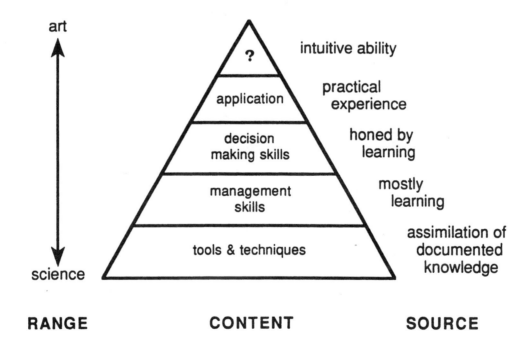

Figure D.1. Range of Project Management Learning

Thoughts provoked by V. Ulimanis, PMI/INTERNET Symposium, Atlanta, 1989.
Reported by I. Wirth, Chairman, and Trudy Stone

The classroom lecture lends itself best to the study of project management tools, but is ineffective for the study of behavioral subjects (e.g., leadership, power, and politics). The "Pre-published" cases (e.g., Harvard case studies) generally are outdated by the time they reach the classroom, although such may well provide a constructive extension of the lecture mode to exercise project management tools and techniques under arbitrary circumstances. The "ongoing" (or live) case study is an alternative to assure up-to-date circumstances, but is then necessarily industry-specific.

Simulation is an attempt to reproduce in the classroom the real socio-economic environment of project management, and can embrace interorganizational affairs, including owner-contractor relations and project performance. Computer programming can be used to control the learning environment. "Role playing" is another form of classroom simulation, used to study interpersonal relationships and small group dynamics, important in both the single project and the "matrix" organization.

On-the-job training (OJT) is a most common method of instruction. It is conducted at the project site, and is obviously industry-specific. It provides the student/practitioner the best opportunity both to put into use some of the project management tools and techniques acquired in earlier forms of learning, as well as gain first-hand experience of the real world of project management.

---

1. Afterthoughts by V. Ulmanis At PMI/INTERNET Symposium, Atlanta, 1989, reported by I. Wirth.
2. Abstracted from I. Wirth, Program Design in Project Management Education: A Road Map, *PM NETwork*, May 1990, p39.

Appendix E

A Glossary Of General Project Management Terminology

Note: The project context is implicit throughout the following definitions.

Accountability. Being answerable for results.

Amount at Stake. The extent of adverse consequences which could occur to the project.

Area of Project Application. The environment in which a project takes place, with its own particular culture, nomenclature and accepted practices.

Authority. One who is vested with power to give final endorsement, which requires no further approval.

Baseline. Management plan and/or scope document fixed at a specific point in time in the project life cycle.

Change. The substitution of one thing in place of another.

Commitment. An agreement to consign or reserve the necessary resources to fulfill a requirement until expenditure occurs. A commitment is an event.

Contract/Procurement Management. The function through which resources are acquired for the project in order to produce the end requirements. Contract/procurement includes both internal (informal) commitments and external (formal) contracts for people, services, materials and equipment.

Control (Rev). Planning, monitoring accomplishment, and exercising any necessary corrective action to yield the required outcome.

Corporate Business Life Cycle. A life cycle which encompasses phases of policy-planning and identification-of-needs which occur before a project is launched, as well as product-in-service and disposal after the project life cycle is completed.

Cost. The cash value of project activity

Cost Management. The function required to maintain effective financial control of the project throughout its life cycle.

Effort. The application of human energy to accomplish an objective.

Environment. The combined internal and external forces, both individual and collective which assist or restrict the attainment of the project objectives.

Executive Authority. The individual or collective body representing the source of project management's authority. This authority may be channeled through a project sponsor, or project director.

Executive Control Point. One or more points in the project life cycle at which the project's executive may exercise a go/no-go decision on the continuation of project activities.

Facilities/Product Life Cycle. A life cycle which encompasses the project life cycle as well as the phases of operation and disposal.

Feedback. Information (data) extracted from a process or situation and used in controlling (directly) or in planning or modifying immediate or future inputs (actions or decisions) into the process or situation.

Forecast. An estimate and prediction of future conditions and events based on information and knowledge available at the time of the forecast.

Function. (i.e., project management function) The series of processes by which the project objectives in that particular area of project management (e.g., scope, quality, time, etc.) are achieved.

Human Resources Management. The function of directing and coordinating human resources throughout the life of the project by applying the art and science of behavioral and administrative knowledge to achieve the predetermined project objectives of scope, quality, time, cost, and participant satisfaction.

Information/Communications Management. The proper organization and control of information transmitted by whatever means to satisfy the needs of the project.

Management. The process of planning, organizing, executing, coordinating, monitoring, forecasting and exercising control.

Monitoring. The capture, analysis and reporting of actual performance compared to planned performance.

Participant. See stakeholder.

Plan. An intended future course of action

Process. The set of activities by means of which an output is achieved.

Professionalism. Being part of a body of people engaged in a superior calling.

Program Management. The management of a series of related projects designed to accomplish broad goals, to which the individual projects contribute, and typically executed over an extended period of time.

Project. Any undertaking with a defined starting point and defined objectives by which completion is identified. In practice, most projects depend on finite or limited resources by which the objectives are to be accomplished.

Project Brief. A major document typically prepared as the basis for an executive management go/no-go decision at an executive control point. Following a go decision, the document becomes the baseline or control basis for the project control cycle.

Project Control Cycle. The sequence of activities which are used to steer the project towards conformance with project requirements — see control.

Project Integration. The bringing together of diverse organizations, groups or parts to form a cohesive whole to successfully achieve project objectives.

Project Life Cycle. The four sequential phases in time through which any project passes: namely, concept, development, execution (implementation or operation), and finishing (termination or close out). Note that these phases may be further broken down into stages which typically reflect the area of project application.

Project Management. The art of directing and coordinating human and material resources throughout the life of a project by using modern management techniques to achieve predetermined objectives of scope, quality, time, cost, and participant satisfaction.

Project Management Body of Knowledge (PMBOK). All subject areas covered in sufficient depth to understand and apply sound project management principles and practices necessary for the successful planning and accomplishment of projects. The generic PMBOK encompasses generally accepted "good project management".

Project Management Institute (PMI). A non-profit organization dedicated to advancing the state-of-the-art in the profession of project management

Project Management Integration. The harmonizing of the four core project management functions of scope, quality, time and cost, through the four facilitating functions of risk, human resources, contract/procurement and information/communications, for purposes of satisfying the project's stakeholders. Scope and quality reflect the technical requirements of the project.

Project Manager. The individual appointed with responsibility for project management of the project.

Project Organization. The orderly structuring of project participants.

Project Phase. The division of a project time frame (or project life cycle) into the largest logical collection of related activities.

Project Stage. A subset of Project Phase.

Project Success. The achievement of stakeholder satisfaction.

Project Team. The central management group headed by a project manager and responsible for the management and successful outcome of the project.

Public Relations. An activity designed to improve the environment in which an organization operates in order to improve the performance of that organization.

Quality (Rev). The composite of all attributes or characteristics, including performance, of an item or product required to satisfy stated or implied needs. Conformance to requirements.

Quality Assurance (Rev). The planned and systematic (managerial) actions necessary to provide adequate confidence that the item or product will satisfy given quality requirements.

Quality Control (Rev). The operational (technical) activities and techniques required to ensure that quality requirements have been fulfilled.

Quality Management. The function required to determine and implement quality policy throughout the project life cycle. Quality management encompasses the sub-functions of Quality Assurance and Quality Control.

Responsibility. The duties, assignments, and accountability for results associated with a designated position in the organization.

Risk (Project Risk). The cumulative effect of the chances of certain occurrences which will adversely affect project objectives. It is the degree of exposure to negative events and their probable consequences.

Risk Management. The art and science of identifying, analyzing and responding to risk factors throughout the life of a project and in the best interests of its objectives.

S Curve. A plot of cumulative progress against time, which, in practice, typically follows the shape of the letter "S."

Schedule. A display of project time allocation.

Scope (Rev). The bounded set of verifiable end products, or outputs, which the project team undertakes to provide to the project sponsor. The required set of end results or products with specified physical or functional characteristics

Scope Management. The function of developing and maintaining project scope.

Sponsor. The generic name given to the source of the project manager's authority. The sponsor may be owner, financier, client etc., or their delegate—see Executive Authority.

Status.   The condition of the project at a specified point in time.

Stakeholder. One who has a stake or interest in the outcome of the project.

System.   A methodical assembly of actions or things forming a logical and connected scheme or unit.

Technique. Skilled means to an end.

Tetrad Trade-off. The graphical representation of the need to balance the objectives (or constraints) of scope, quality, time and cost.

Time.   The measure of duration.

Time Management. The function required to maintain appropriate allocation of time to the overall conduct of the project through the successive phases of its life cycle.

Uncertainty. The possibility that events may occur which will impact the project either favorably or unfavorably. See also (project) Risk.

Work.   The exertion of human energy

Work Breakdown. A task-oriented "family tree" of activities which organizes, defines and graphically displays the total work to be accomplished in order to achieve the final objectives of the project.

YOUR COMMENTS
on
A Framework for Project and Program Management Integration

HELP US HELP YOU!

So that we may better provide you with the practical information you need, please take a moment to record your comments on this page and return it to:

The Executive Director
Project Management Institute
130 South State Road
Upper Darby, PA 19082

I/we have the following suggestions regarding this handbook:_____

_____

_____

_____

_____

_____

_____

_____

_____

_____

_____

_____

_____

_____

_____

_____

_____

_____

_____

_____

_____

Name_____

Address_____

City_____State_____ZIP Code_____

Country_____Date_____

R. Max Wideman, *P.Eng. FEIC, FICE, Fellow PMI, is a professional engineer specializing in project management consulting. Since graduating at London University, his experience has included hydroelectric, river, marine, transportation, industrial, institutional, commercial and residential projects. He has also been instrumental in social and environmental impact studies, major contract and expropriation claims, construction productivity, and project management audit. In working for a diversity of sectors, he has gained a broad perspective and insight into the project management process.*

Mr. Wideman has lectured extensively, presenting papers or seminars on a variety of project management topics in Canada, China, Egypt, Iceland, India, Jamaica, Pakistan, the Philippines, Saudi Arabia, the United Kingdom, and the USA.

In 1974, Mr. Wideman joined the Project Management Institute (PMI) and later launched the PMI West Coast BC chapter. In 1982 he was elected to the International Board as Vice President Member Services and served as director for three years. During this time, he was assigned responsibility for expanding and codifying PMI's existing standards of knowledge by conducting a major voluntary study by PMI members. The resulting report became known as the Project Management Body of Knowledge, or "PMBOK," which was approved by the PMI Board in March 1987.

Mr. Wideman received PMI's Distinguished Contribution to Project Management Award in 1985, and the following year was honored as PMI Person-of-the-Year. He was elected PMI president for 1987, became chairman in 1988, and was made a Fellow of the Institute in 1989. Mr. Wideman has authored a number of articles and papers for the Institute's publications and is author of <u>Cost Control of Capital Projects</u>, AEW Services, Vancouver, 1983.

Code of Ethics
for
The Project Management Profession

PREAMBLE: Project Management Professionals, in the pursuit of the profession, affect the quality of life for all people in our society. Therefore, it is vital that Project Management Professionals conduct their work in an ethical manner to earn and maintain the confidence of team members, colleagues, employees, employers, clients and the public.

ARTICLE I: Project Management Professionals shall maintain high standards of personal and professional conduct, and:

a. Accept responsibility for their actions.

b. Undertake projects and accept responsibility only if qualified by training or experience, or after full disclosure to their employers or clients of pertinent qualifications.

c. Maintain their professional skills at the state of the art and recognize the importance of continued personal development and education.

d. Advance the integrity and prestige of the profession by practicing in a dignified manner.

e. Support this code and encourage colleagues and co-workers to act in accordance with this code.

f. Support the professional society by actively participating and encouraging colleagues and co-workers to participate.

g. Obey the laws of the country in which work is being performed.

ARTICLE II: Project Management Professionals shall, in their work:

a. Provide the necessary project leadership to promote maximum productivity while striving to minimize costs.

b. Apply state of the art project management tools and techniques to ensure quality, cost and time objectives, as set forth in the project plan, are met.

c. Treat fairly all project team members, colleagues and co-workers, regardless of race, religion, sex, age or national origin.

d. Protect project team members from physical and mental harm.

e. Provide suitable working conditions and opportunities for project team members.

f. Seek, accept and offer honest criticism of work, and properly credit the contribution of others.

g. Assist project team members, colleagues and co-workers in their professional development.

ARTICLE III: Project Management Professionals shall, in their relations with employers and clients:

a. Act as faithful agents or trustees for their employers and clients in professional or business matters.

b. Keep information on the business affairs or technical processes of an employer or client in confidence while employed, and later, until such information is properly released.

c. Inform their employers, clients, professional societies or public agencies of which they are members or to which they may make any presentations, of any circumstance that could lead to a conflict of interest.

d. Neither give nor accept, directly or indirectly, any gift, payment or service of more than nominal value to or from those having business relationships with their employers or clients.

e. Be honest and realistic in reporting project quality, cost and time.

ARTICLE IV: Project Management Professionals shall, in fulfilling their responsibilities to the community:

a. Protect the safety, health and welfare of the public and speak out against abuses in these areas affecting the public interest.

b. Seek to extend public knowledge and appreciation of the project management profession and its achievements.